LABOR RELATIONS AND PUBLIC POLICY SERIES

No. 28

(MAJOR INDUSTRIAL RESEARCH UNIT STUDY No. 64)

DEREGULATION AND THE DECLINE OF THE UNIONIZED TRUCKING INDUSTRY

by

CHARLES R. PERRY

with the assistance of

CRAIG M. WARING

PE

INDUSTRIAL RESEARCH UNIT
The Wharton School
University of Pennsylvania
Philadelphia, Pennsylvania 19104-6358

Foreword

In 1968, the Industrial Research Unit inaugurated its Labor Relations and Public Policy Series as a means of examining issues and stimulating discussions in the complex and controversial areas of collective bargaining and the regulation of labor-management disputes. Thus far, twenty-nine monographs have been published in this series. Eleven of these deal with various policies and procedures of the National Labor Relations Board. The other eighteen cover such significant issues as collective bargaining in the 1970s; welfare and strikes; opening the skilled construction trades to blacks; the Davis-Bacon Act; the labor-management situation in urban school systems; old age, handicapped, and Vietnam-era antidiscrimination legislation; the impact of the Occupational Safety and Health Act; the Landrum-Griffin Act; the effects of the AT&T-EEO consent decree; union's rights to company information; employee relations and regulation; operating during strikes; union violence and the law; the impact of antitrust legislation on employee relations; prevailing wage legislation; and comparable worth theory and practice.

This study, *Deregulation and the Decline of Unionized Trucking*, is twenty-eighth in the series, and is also one of a series of major studies published by the Wharton Industrial Research Unit analyzing employee relations in industries in which unions are declining or have never gained strength. The International Brotherhood of Teamsters, Chauffeurs, Warehousemen and Helpers of America, now the largest union in North America, has seen its core of strength decimated by deregulation, which has broken Teamster dominance in the trucking industry and has allowed nonunion truckers to move into a major share of the business. The situation that Professor Charles R. Perry and his associates describe and analyze is a classic story of how government regulation enhances union power by preventing competition in an industry, and how unions and the unionized sector are hurt when deregulation restores competition.

The study was begun by Craig M. Waring in 1981. Prior to his enrollment in the Wharton Master of Business Administration (M.B.A.) program, he had researched trucking industry problems and was aware of the changes occurring in the industry's labor relations. Unfortunately, he was unable to complete a draft before he graduated and accepted a position in industry.

After fulfilling prior commitments, Professor Perry, who is both a faculty member in the Wharton Department of Management and a Senior Faculty Research Associate in the Wharton Industrial Research Unit, assumed the task. Difficulties in obtaining and processing data, particularly the key statistics from the Interstate Commerce Commission, delayed the completion of the project, but these data do provide significant hard information concerning the impact of deregulation on unionized carriers and the Teamsters union. Supplemental data include responses to questionnaires developed by Mr. Waring, which were sent in slightly different forms to both the for-hire and the private segments of the industry.

The book marks another in a series of significant publications by Dr. Perry, which includes *The Impact of Negotiations in Public Education* (1973), *The Impact of Government Manpower Programs* (1975), *The Impact of OSHA* (1978), *Operating During Strikes* (1982), and *Collective Bargaining and the Decline of the United Mine Workers* (1984), plus several first-rate journal articles. Professor Perry's research was aided not only by the earlier work of Mr. Waring, but also by the able assistance of Peter N. Glick, one of the few exceptional undergraduates who qualified for a research position in the Industrial Research Unit; Michael V. Nguyen, who received his M.B.A. in May 1985; Erik B. Halverson, a student in the Moore School of Electrical Engineering, University of Pennsylvania, who handled most of the data processing work; Cindy W. Drankowski, who, like Messrs. Waring and Nguyen, is in industry after earning a Wharton M.B.A.; and Amie D. Thornton, who is currently a student in the joint M.B.A.-J.D. program of the University of Pennsylvania Law School and the Wharton School. The manuscript was word processed by Cynthia K. Smith, Sherrie L. Waitsman, Rita M. Gorman, and O.P. Suri, and was edited by Barbara A. Kimmelman and Christopher B. Mario of the Industrial Research Unit's editorial staff under the direction of Kate C. Bradford, chief editor. Ms. Kimmelman also prepared the index. Marthenia A. Perrin, office manager, supervised administrative matters relating to the project.

Initial support for the study came from a grant supplied by the Carthage Foundation, through the courtesy and interest of its treasurer, Richard M. Larry. Further support was provided by the Industrial Research Unit's Research Advisory Group, and by the generous annual grants of the J. Howard Pew Freedom Trust in support of the Labor Relations and Public Policy Series. The very supportive Pew Trust grants also underwrote publication costs. The interest in our work by Robert J. Smith, President, Fred H. Billups, Jr., Vice-President, and Robert G. Dunlop, Member, Board of Directors, as well as the staff of the Glenmede Trust Company, which administers the Pew foundations, is most heartening and much appreciated.

As in all works published by the Industrial Research Unit, the author is solely responsible for the research and for all opinions expressed, none of which should be attributed to the grantors or to the University of Pennsylvania.

HERBERT R. NORTHRUP, Director
Industrial Research Unit
The Wharton School
University of Pennsylvania

Philadelphia
January 1986

TABLE OF CONTENTS

LIST OF TABLES

CHAPTER I

Introduction

The trucking industry is a large and vital element of the nation's intercity freight transportation system. In 1980, truck transport accounted for almost one-quarter of the volume of intercity freight and represented two-thirds of the intercity freight bill in the United States.[1] Given these figures, it is hardly surprising that in passing the Motor Carrier Act (MCA) of 1980, the Congress declared that "a safe, sound, competitive and fuel efficient motor carrier system is vital to the maintenance of a strong national economy and a strong national defense."[2]

The trucking industry also occupies a salient place in the nation's labor relations system. The International Brotherhood of Teamsters (IBT), more commonly known simply as the Teamsters, is the nation's largest union, and is also one of the most powerful by virtue of its control over the movement of freight by truck. For the past two decades the central element in that control has been the multi-employer (industry-wide) bargaining system constructed and protected by the union for the purpose of negotiating a National Master Freight Agreement (NMFA).

The first NMFA was negotiated in 1964 and gave the Teamsters what the first National Bituminous Coal Wage Agreement gave the United Mine Workers in 1950—a vehicle for controlling and managing an industry prone to ruinous competition if left to its own devices.[3] In both cases the industries in question relinquished control in exchange for the hope or promise that the union would take and keep labor out of competition by organizing to the extent of the market and/or imposing standardized terms and conditions on all operators, whether by legal or extra-legal means. In theory, both

---

[1] Transportation Policy Associates, *Supplements, Updates and Corrections to Transportation in America* (Washington, D.C.: Transportation Policy Associates, 1984), pp. 4, 6.

[2] Motor Carrier Act of 1980, Pub. L. No. 96-296, 94 Stat. 793.

[3] For information on the United Mine Workers and the changing character of the coal industry see Charles R. Perry, *Collective Bargaining and the Decline of the United Mine Workers*, Major Industrial Research Unit Studies No. 60 (Philadelphia: Wharton Industrial Research Unit, University of Pennsylvania, 1984).

industries gained a measure of bargaining power by reducing their individual vulnerability to a strike and thereby reducing their collective vulnerability to whipsawing. In fact, however, that benefit appears to have been more illusory than real in both cases because of constraints on the willingness (coal) or ability (trucking) of operators to withstand the economic costs of even a multi-employer strike.

The most compelling difference between coal and trucking in their ventures into multi-employer bargaining is the competitive environment in the two industries. In the 1950s, coal was an unregulated and unprotected industry confronted with the prospect of ruinous competition not only within the industry but with other energy sources. By contrast, in the 1960s trucking was a regulated and protected industry confronted with the prospect of no competition either within the industry or from other modes of transport. In the absence of the prospect and/or reality of both intra- and inter-industry competition, it seems unlikely that management would have a strong incentive to control or reduce labor costs.

The special competitive circumstances of the trucking industry changed dramatically with the passage of the MCA in 1980. That act, which deregulated the industry, brought an end to much of the protective regulation that had spared those in the industry the bother of competition for over forty years, and opened the way for a potential rebirth of the ruinous competition that preceded regulation. Should such competition emerge, it clearly would greatly enhance management's incentive to control and reduce labor costs, particularly in a relatively labor-intensive industry such as trucking. The result of such competition would be growing pressure on management to put labor back into competition by seeking wage or workrule concessions from the union, or by pursuing the option of nonunion operation.

The possibility that deregulation would force the industry to mount a concerted campaign to dismantle or circumvent the Teamsters' NMFA bargaining system and structure was recognized by the union long before 1980, and was reflected in their opposition to the MCA of 1980 and, quite probably, in their endorsement of Ronald Reagan in the 1980 presidential election. The fact that the union has continued to criticize deregulation and to oppose further deregulation clearly suggests that at least some of its fears proved justified, although the union itself has admitted to being unsure about the extent to which its setbacks in trucking in the early 1980s were a product of deregulation, as opposed to the coincident recession.

THE IMPACT OF DEREGULATION

Deregulation provides an excellent opportunity to study the ramifications of a change in the competitive character of an industry on the character of its labor relations system, because the competitive change is sudden rather than gradual, as is the need for adaptation to that change. In that context, the deregulation of trucking is no exception, and may indeed be of special interest for two reasons. First, because deregulation coincided with a recession, added pressure should have been exerted on management and labor to quickly identify and implement adaptive responses to their changed circumstances. Second, because the Teamsters should be able to organize to the extent of the market in trucking without having to deal with foreign competition, added insight should be gained into the ability of a union to veto changes in the law of supply and demand by virtue of its organizing and bargaining power.

The effect of regulation was to limit entry into, and price competition in, the trucking industry. Deregulation, therefore, should have the opposite effect of encouraging entry into, and price competition in, the industry, but only to the extent that it promises to be profitable given the organizing and bargaining power of the Teamsters. In that context, it is possible to distinguish three patterns of potential effects of deregulation based on the extent to which Teamster control is substitutable for government regulation in effectively discouraging entry and price competition.

It is conceivable that the power of the Teamsters to set and enforce terms and conditions of employment on an industry-wide basis could perpetuate the effects of regulation. To the extent that the union's bargaining power were sufficient to enable it to expropriate any excess profits of trucking firms attributable to regulation, incentives to enter the industry would remain weak as long as potential entrants had reason to fear the union's organizing power and/or to anticipate that they could not escape paying union wages. If the union indeed were able to organize or standardize the entire industry, it would fix about two-thirds of total operating costs and would thereby dramatically reduce the latitude for price competition.

On the other hand, it is possible that the organizing and bargaining power of the Teamsters would be totally inadequate to fill the void left by deregulation. That would be the case if, despite the union's bargaining power, there were monopoly profits to be made in the industry to encourage entry, particularly if potential entrants had no reason to fear the union's organizing power or to anticipate paying union wages. In that situation, it seems likely that new entrants would so flood the industry as to undermine the ability of the union to maintain any semblance of a union wage or pretense of keeping labor out of competition.

Finally, there is the inevitable middle ground between the union and nonunion outcomes of deregulation. This outcome model suggests that the combination of past and prospective Teamster organizing and bargaining power is sufficiently awesome to discourage some, but not all, potential entrants to the industry, and to encourage most, but not all, operators to conform to union standards. Like any average, it may reflect either the condition of a substantial portion of the population in question or the halfway point between two widely divided segments of that population. The latter possibility cannot be ignored when dealing with the trucking industry, given the complexity of the operations it encompasses and the number of ways in which those operations can be grouped in juxtaposed pairs, such as: 1) common and contract carriers; 2) regular and irregular route carriers; 3) general freight and special commodity carriers; and 4) less-than-truckload lot and truckload lot carriers.

FOCUS AND METHODOLOGY OF THIS STUDY

The ultimate goal of this investigation of the trucking industry and its industrial relations system is to determine which of these models of the outcome of deregulation best fits the trucking industry and/or its major constituent elements. The first step in that process must be an understanding of the industry and its industrial relations system as they entered into, evolved during, and emerged from their prolonged period of protective regulation by the Interstate Commerce Commission (ICC). The second step is to document the basic economic changes in the industry produced by deregulation, and to determine the pattern of the effects of those changes within the industry. The final step is to project the long-term effects of deregulation on the trucking industry and to speculate about the implications of those effects for the future course of labor relations in the industry.

There is an abundance of institutional, economic, and legal literature on the history of the trucking industry prior to its deregulation in 1980. That body of literature will be drawn on selectively to describe the economic and regulatory constraints within which the industry's labor relations system evolved prior to deregulation. No attempt will be made to provide a detailed legal or economic analysis of the direct and/or indirect effects of deregulation on the labor relations of the industry. Instead, special attention will be focused on the various assessments of the economic and institutional effects of regulation on labor relations presented during the debate over deregulation.

There is also an ample body of literature on the history of labor relations in the trucking industry. Outstanding within that body of literature are Garnel's study, *The Rise of Teamster Power in the West*,[4] and James and James' book, *Hoffa and the Teamsters: A Study of Union Power*,[5] both of which will be drawn on extensively in describing the development of the industry's labor relations system. Relatively little scholarly attention has been paid to trucking industry labor relations since the signing of the first NMFA in 1964. Notable exceptions to that rule are three works by Levinson, the most recent being his article "Trucking," in *Collective Bargaining: Contemporary American Experience*,[6] that constitute a valuable source of information regarding the course of the industry's labor relations between 1964 and the advent of deregulation.

The prospect and process of deregulation produced a flood of studies, statements, and speculations regarding the short-term impact and/or long-term implications of that action for the industry and its industrial relations system. Management, union, and government each presented its own view of the benefits and costs associated with the return to free competition in the intercity motor freight market. For the most part, these self-serving statements were far more theoretical than empirical, primarily because there were only preliminary and/or superficial data available on the actual consequences of deregulation. However flawed such statements/predictions may have been, they are not without value in understanding the short-term impact of deregulation and anticipating the long-term implications of that action.

There are numerous sources of statistical data on the trucking industry, including the Interstate Commerce Commission (ICC), the Bureau of Labor Statistics (BLS), and the industry's various orga-

---

[4] Donald Garnel, *The Rise of Teamster Power in the West* (Berkeley, California: University of California Press, 1972).

[5] Ralph C. James and Estelle Dinerstein James, *Hoffa and the Teamsters: A Study in Union Power* (Princeton, N.J.: D. Van Nostrand and Company, 1965).

[6] Harold M. Levinson, "Trucking" in *Collective Bargaining: Contemporary American Experience*, ed. Gerald G. Somers (Madison, Wis.: Industrial Research Association, 1980), pp. 99-149. See also Harold M. Levinson, *Determining Forces in Collective Bargaining* (New York: John Wiley and Sons, 1966), pp. 215-56; and Harold M. Levinson, "Collective Bargaining and Technological Change in the Trucking Industry," in *Collective Bargaining and Technological Change in American Transportation* (Evanston, Ill.: The Transportation Center at Northwestern University, 1971), pp. 4-84.

nizations, such as American Trucking Associations (ATA), Trucking Employers Inc. (TEI), and the IBT. Unfortunately, such data are based on different sets or subsets of trucking firms, making it difficult to integrate available data into a comprehensive statistical picture of the industry. This problem is particularly significant in a study of the relationship of regulation and labor relations because available data are structured around either one or the other of these overlapping but not coextensive systems.

The key variables for the purposes of this study are the level and trend of unionization in regulated trucking. The best source of data on regulated trucking is the ICC, which annually publishes extensive information on the operations of regulated carriers as well as detailed reports of its regulatory actions. Such sources of information provide a basis for tracing the overall economic and regulatory course of the regulated trucking industry, but not its labor relations. In order to fill that void, it was necessary to secure access to the ICC's data base and to devise a means of differentiating union and nonunion carriers. The ICC was able and willing to provide access to the individual carrier operating data, which Class I and II carriers are required to report annually, for 1974-1983 in the case of Class I carriers, and 1977-1983 in the case of Class II carriers. Among the operating data that carriers must report are total contributions to health, welfare, and pension funds. Unionized carriers are required by contract to make such contributions in specified amounts per week per employee; nonunion carriers are not and do not. Thus, it was possible to use this variable on a per employee basis to determine the extent to which a reporting carrier was unionized, and then to reaggregate the data in terms of number of carriers, number of employees, and operating variables such as gross revenue, payroll, and benefit cost.

In an effort to gain additional insight into the relationship between regulation and labor relations in the regulated segment of the industry, a questionnaire regarding changes in operations undertaken in anticipation of, or in reaction to, deregulation was sent to approximately 3,500 common carriers. At the same time, a similar questionnaire was sent to a like number of private carriers in an effort to gain insight into the extent to which deregulation had or would alter their trucking operations. (A copy of the questions asked is included as an appendix.) The rate of return of both questionnaires was approximately 10 percent.

The basic focus of the study is on the efforts of management, government, and the Teamsters to control the tendencies of the trucking industry toward ruinous competition and competitive chaos. Since management is not in a position, legally or economically, to control the industry on its own, that task fell to the government (with respect to routes and rates) and the union (with respect to workrules and wage rates).

The basic framework of the study is historical and centers on the rise and fall of control over the industry's self-destructive tendencies. There are two possible perspectives on the ebb and flow of competition in trucking. The first and most obvious focuses on the role of government in controlling the competitive urges of present and prospective participants in the industry. In this view, the turning point in the industry's condition would be the deregulation of 1980. A second and more subtle perspective acknowledges the role of the union as a partner to the government in controlling the competitive urges of present and prospective participants in the industry by virtue of its power to enforce union standards on all such participants. In this view, the turning point in the industry's condition came shortly after the conclusion of the first NMFA, when the economic control of the IBT over the industry began to weaken. It is the latter view around which this study is organized.

Chapters two through five deal with the rise of control that began with the passage of the Motor Carrier Act of 1935 and ended with the signing of the first NMFA in 1964. The first three of these chapters deal with the actors in the system: management, government, and union. The fourth is a transitional chapter that deals with the character and course of the collective bargaining relationship between management and union between 1964 and 1980.

The four chapters that follow deal with the decline of control that began in the mid-1960s, when the power of the IBT peaked, and ended with the deregulation of the industry in 1980. Again, the first three of these chapters deal with the actors in the system: union, government, and management. The fourth deals with the emergent shape and structure of the industry's labor relations system after deregulation.

The final chapter is reserved for extrapolation and speculation about the future of the trucking industry, of the Teamsters union, and of the relationship between the two. That is no easy matter, given the complexity of the industry and the union. It is further complicated by the central but uncertain role that the government seems likely to play in the fate of both the industry and the union.

CHAPTER II

The Trucking Industry

The American trucking industry celebrated its eightieth anniversary in 1983. Although the first trucks appeared on city streets around 1900, they found little immediate acceptance, and by 1903 "only a few city stores and a St. Louis newspaper [had] changed from horse and wagon delivery to truck."[1] In May of that year, America's first commercial vehicle contest was held in New York City to test the viability of trucks in commercial use. Breakdowns, accidents, and delays notwithstanding, "the mercantile world came away convinced trucks were a transportation force to be reckoned with"[2] and a new industry was born.

THE GROWTH OF TRUCKING

The mercantile world indeed found trucks a force to be reckoned with. In 1904, there were fewer than 500 trucks registered in the United States.[3] By 1908, that number had grown eightfold, to 4,000, and by 1916 had done so again to 300,000.[4] By the time the industry reached its eightieth anniversary there were approximately 35 million trucks registered in the United States.[5]

The Early Years

The growth of trucking prior to the end of World War I was confined to local cartage. Doubts about the "economy, reliability, durability, speed and carrying capacity" of trucks limited their attractiveness for commercial use to "city deliveries and hauling freight between railroad terminals."[6] By the end of the war, how-

---

[1] Gary M. LaBella, *A Glance Back* (Washington, D.C.: American Trucking Associations, 1977), p. 6.

[2] *Ibid.*, p. 8.

[3] Parker McCollester, *Federal Motor Carrier Regulation* (New York: Traffic Publishing Company, 1935), p. 4.

[4] LaBella, *A Glance Back*, p. 9.

[5] Transportation Policy Associates, *Transportation in America: A Statistical Analysis of Transportation in the United States* (Washington, D.C.: Transportation Policy Associates, March 1983), p. 33.

[6] LaBella, *A Glance Back*, pp. 7, 42.

ever, the combination of poor roads, solid tires, low speed, and limited size, which had precluded effective use of trucks in the intercity freight market, began to break down as a result of improvements in both the nation's roads and in automotive engineering, coupled with the advent of pneumatic tires and the semi-trailer.

In the 1920s, trucks consolidated their hold on the local delivery and cartage markets and began to invade the intercity freight market on a limited (short-haul) basis. By the mid-1920s, the state of the nation's roads and automotive technology had progressed to the point of affording trucks two potential competitive advantages over the railroads in the short-haul intercity movement of freight: speed and flexibility. Those advantages would have been more than offset by the railroads' lower cost per ton-mile were it not for the railroads' practice of basing rates on the value of the commodity transported rather than the cost of transporting the commodity. Thus, truckers could and did use cost-of-service pricing to compete with the railroads for the business of shippers of high-value commodities.

There was no shortage of truckers willing to avail themselves of the opportunities in the intercity freight market created by improved roads and vehicles. The trucking business was easy to enter. Both capital and skill requirements were minimal, and other than licensing and registration fees there were no operating restrictions on entrants to the industry. Thus, the latter half of the 1920s witnessed growing competition between trucks and trains in the intercity freight market, to which the railroads responded with a publicity campaign focused on truck safety problems and a lobbying effort for state and federal laws to restrict motor carrier operations.[7]

The advent of the Great Depression intensified the competition between the railroad and trucking industries in the intercity freight market. It also produced growing competition within the trucking industry in that same market. The railroad industry was the most obvious loser in that environment, as shippers sought speed and flexibility in the interest of reducing inventory costs. The large, established trucking firms were also losers, as they found their rates being undercut by small truckers who, knowing or caring little about hours, safety, or rate of return, were willing to engage in cutthroat competition.[8]

The railroads' response to heightened competition in the 1930s was to intensify its campaign of the 1920s for restrictions on motor carriage and to focus that campaign at the federal level. The large, established firms in the trucking industry, which had fought the

---

[7] John J. George, *Motor Carrier Regulation in the United States* (Spartanburg, S.C.: Band and White, 1929), pp. 5-7.

[8] LaBella, *A Glance Back*, p. 18.

railroads' demands for government regulation in the 1920s, allied themselves with the railroads in making such demands in the 1930s because they perceived that competition had reached the point where "trucking was unstable and chaotic and in desperate need of some order."[9]

The passage of the National Industrial Recovery Act (NIRA) in 1933 offered the large, established trucking firms an opportunity to impose order on the industry's chaos. They responded quickly by forming the American Trucking Associations (ATA) for the purpose of unifying the industry and writing a code of fair competition for it.[10] The ATA submitted a code of fair competition to the National Recovery Administration in February 1934 under which "every for-hire trucking company was required to register, . . to observe maximum hours of labor and minimum rates of pay, . . [and] to file a 'schedule of minima for rates and tariff.' "[11] When the NIRA was declared unconstitutional in 1935, that code became null and void, but the industry was spared a return to instability and chaos when

> Joseph B. Eastman, federal coordinator of transportation and a great friend of the motor carrier industry, drafted a regulatory bill that provided for . . . the economic regulation of for-hire carriers under the authority of the Interstate Commerce Commission.[12]

That bill became law as the Motor Carrier Act (MCA) of 1935, which gave the Interstate Commerce Commission (ICC) regulatory authority over motor freight carriage and a mandate to use that authority to "promote adequate, economical and efficient service by motor carriers, and reasonable charges therefor, without unjust discrimination, undue preferences or advantages, and unfair or destructive competitive practices."[13] The passage of the MCA of 1935 brought an end to ruinous competition within the trucking industry, and for the the next forty-five years, until the passage of the MCA of 1980, established trucking firms were spared the hazards of easy entry and rate cutting by the protective regulation of a benevolent ICC determined to fulfill its mandate to prevent destructive competitive practices.

The Postwar Years

Since 1950, trucking has been characterized by substantial and sustained long-term growth. The demand for freight transportation service has grown with the growth of the economy, and trucking

---

[9] *Ibid.*
[10] *Ibid.*, p. 20.
[11] *Ibid.*
[12] *Ibid.*
[13] Motor Carrier Act of 1935, chapter 498, 49 Stat. 543, section 202a.

has enjoyed more than its share of that growth in demand (see Table II-1). Between 1950 and 1960, the volume of intercity truck freight movement increased by approximately 65 percent. About one-third of that increase in volume came about as a result of increasing demand for intercity freight service, the remaining two-thirds as a result of trucking's growing share of intercity freight traffic. Since 1960, the industry's market share has grown only slightly, resulting in more modest rates of volume growth: 45 percent between 1960 and 1970 and 35 percent between 1970 and 1980.

The growth of the trucking industry since 1950 has produced a substantial increase in total trucking employment, from about 500,000 in 1950 to 1,000,000 in 1980 (see Table II-1). There are two noteworthy aspects of the pattern of employment growth between 1950 and 1980. First, growth in total employment (100 percent) fell

TABLE II-1

The Growth of the Trucking Industry 1950–1984

Year	Intercity Ton-Miles (Billions)		Employment (Thousands) Number
	Number	Percent of U.S. Total	
1950	173	16.3	557
1955	223	17.5	688
1960	285	21.8	770
1965	359	21.9	882
1970	412	21.3	998
1971	445	22.8	995
1972	470	22.7	1043
1973	505	22.6	1096
1974	495	22.4	1102
1975	454	22.0	1024
1976	510	23.2	1068
1977	555	24.1	1132
1978	599	24.3	1212
1979	608	23.6	1249
1980	555	22.3	1189
1981	527	21.7	1168
1982	520	23.1	1128
1983	548	23.7	1133
1984	602	23.6	1212

Source: Transportation Policy Associates, *Transportation in America* (Washington, D.C.: Transportation Policy Associates, March 1983), p. 7; *Supplements, Updates and Corrections to Transportation in America* (Washington, D.C.: Transportation Policy Associates, November 1985), p. 6; U.S. Department of Labor, Bureau of Labor Statistics, *Employment, Hours, and Earnings, United States, 1909–1984,* Volume II (Washington, D.C.: Government Printing Office, March 1985), p. 646.

far short of growth in volume (300 percent). Although these two percentages are not based on the same set of trucking activities, they do suggest that the industry has been the beneficiary of long-term productivity gains. Second, most of the growth in the industry over the period occurred between 1950 and 1970. The 1970-1980 period saw not only a slowing in the rate of growth of employment, but the first serious cyclical declines in industry employment: 8 percent between 1973 and 1975, and 11 percent between 1979 and 1982.

The dramatic absolute and relative growth of intercity trucking in the postwar period fundamentally changed the character of the trucking industry. By 1940, trucking's share of the intercity freight market had reached 10 percent,[14] but economically and institutionally trucking continued to be a local industry. By 1960, when trucking's share of that market exceeded 20 percent, this was no longer the case. Economically, intercity traffic accounted for more than one-half of estimated total expenditures for motor freight transport.[15] Institutionally, the industry had been molded into a series of regional structures in part as a consequence of regulation but more importantly by the successful efforts of the Teamsters to build a system of regional bargaining structures. When, in 1964, management and union agreed to superimpose on those regional structures a national bargaining structure in the form of the NMFA, trucking became a national industry.

THE STRUCTURE OF TRUCKING

The movement of freight by truck is done by two statistically distinct types of carriers: for-hire and private. A for-hire carrier is one engaged in the business of transporting freight belonging to someone else. A private carrier is one whose trucking activities are confined to the transport of its own freight as an adjunct to its basic business activities. There are two major technical differences between these types of carriers. First, for-hire carriers are classified statistically as trucking companies and considered part of the trucking industry; private carriers are not and their trucking activities are classified statistically as part of their primary business activity. Second, private carriers typically are not subject to the same detailed regulatory limits on their trucking operations as are for-hire carriers.

---

[14] Transportation Policy Associates, *Transportation in America*, p. 7.
[15] *Ibid.*, pp. 5-7.

The basic focus of this study is for-hire carriers, but that should not obscure the importance of private carriage activity. The fact that private carriers are not classified statistically as part of the trucking industry does not mean that they are not so economically. Private carriage is an alternative to for-hire carriage for most large shippers, and as such, it constitutes a potentially stringent competitive constraint on for-hire trucking firms. Shippers will exercise their option to provide, rather than purchase, trucking service when they perceive that they can secure more cost-effective service using their own equipment and employees than they can by relying on for-hire carriers. There are no data on the number of shippers who have perceived such advantage, but it has been estimated that there were more than 100,000 private carriers in operation at the end of the 1970s.[16]

The movement of freight by for-hire motor carriers takes place in two economically distinct markets: local (intracity) and over-the-road (intercity). Over-the-road trucking involves the movement of freight within an intercity/interstate market where carriers typically are subject to both intermodal competition and federal regulation. Local trucking involves the movement of freight within an intracity/intrastate market where carriers typically are not subject to intermodal competition or federal regulation, although subject to state regulation.

The primary concern of this study is over-the-road trucking, but it must be noted that local cartage historically has been, and continues to be, a vital part of the trucking industry. Both the trucking industry and the Teamsters originated as local institutions and retained that character through much of the first half of this century. Local cartage still accounts for more than 40 percent of all expenditures for motor freight service[17] and approximately 70 to 80 percent of the total trucking industry membership of the Teamsters.[18]

Federal regulation added yet another dichotomy in the classification of motor freight carriers: regulated and exempt. Regulated carriers are those for-hire carriers that must obtain ICC authority to operate. Exempt carriers require no such authority, and include private carriers, local cartage, and for-hire, over-the-road

---

[16] Charles A. Taff, *Commercial Motor Transportation* (Centreville, M.D.: Cornell Maritime Press, 1980), p. 128.

[17] Transportation Policy Associates, *Transportation in America*, p. 4.

[18] Harold M. Levinson, "Trucking," in *Collective Bargaining: Contemporary American Experience,* ed. Gerald G. Somers (Madison, Wis.: Industrial Relations Research Association, 1980), pp. 103-4.

carriers of exempt commodities, primarily unprocessed agricultural products.

Regulated carriers constitute the core of the for-hire, over-the-road trucking industry; they are the central focus of this study. But this focus should not obscure the fact that regulated carriers are a numerical minority in that segment of the trucking industry. In 1977, for example, there were 58,000 exempt for-hire, over-the-road carriers, compared to 16,000 regulated carriers.[19] In that year, however, the operating revenues of regulated carriers totalled more than $31 billion, compared to less than $13 billion for the exempt carriers.[20]

Regulated Carriers

The ICC divides regulated carriers into three classes based on operating revenues. The dollar divisions between the classes have been adjusted periodically. In the late 1970s, Class III carriers were those with revenues of less than $500,000; Class II carriers, those with revenues between $500,000 and $3,000,000; and Class I carriers, those with revenues in excess of $3,000,000. At that time there were approximately 1,000 Class I carriers, 3,000 Class II carriers, and 12,000 Class III carriers. Although Class I carriers represented less than 10 percent of all regulated carriers, they accounted for more than 70 percent of such carriers' total operating revenues.[21]

There are two basic types of regulated carriers: common and contract. Common carriers provide service to the general public and are legally obligated to provide service to any shipper requesting it. Contract carriers do not haul for the general public, but provide specialized service to individual shippers on a long-term contractual basis. Contract carriers historically have constituted a limited segment of the regulated trucking industry, serving the unique needs of individual shippers or groups of shippers with specialized equipment and specific point-to-point service. The number of such carriers was limited further by restrictions imposed by the ICC on the number of shippers that a contract carrier could serve.

---

[19] See Interstate Commerce Commission, *91st Annual Report of the Interstate Commerce Commission, Fiscal Year Ending September 30, 1977* (Washington, D.C.: Government Printing Office, 1977), p. 137, Appendix E; and U.S. Department of Commerce, Bureau of the Census, *1977 Census of Transportation: Nonregulated Motor Carriers and Public Warehousing* (Washington, D.C.: Government Printing Office, April 1984), p. 2, Table 1.

[20] U.S. Bureau of the Census, *1977 Census of Transportation: Nonregulated Motor Carriers*, p. 2, Table 1.

[21] Interstate Commerce Commission, *91st Annual Report, 1977*, p. 137, Appendix E, Table 1.

Common carriers constitute the heart of the regulated trucking industry, both economically and institutionally. In terms of the federal regulatory system, there are two types of common carriers: regular route carriers of general freight and irregular route carriers of special commodities. Regular route carriers operate under ICC authority that specifies the possible points of origin and destinations of freight and the routes over which freight may be carried, but does not specify the types of freight that may be carried. Irregular route carriers operate under ICC authority that specifies the types of freight that may be carried and the geographic areas between which freight may be carried, but not the routes over which it must be carried.

The basic operating characteristics of regular and irregular route carriers are typically quite different. Regular route carriers of general freight operate through terminals where less-than-truckload lot cargoes are received, sorted, and consolidated into truckload lots for movement to other terminals where the process is reversed. Such terminals also serve as points for cargo transfers between carriers (interlining) made necessary by ICC-imposed geographic limits on the operating authority of individual carriers. Irregular route carriers of special commodities typically do not operate through terminals because they can offer point-to-point service whether for truckload or less-than-truckload lots. In that respect, their operations more closely parallel those of contract carriers than those of regular route carriers.

Regular Route Carriers

Regular route carriers of general freight long have been the center of union presence and power within the trucking industry, and it is difficult to understand the labor relations of the industry without understanding the economics of these carriers. Yet because regular route common carriers are a highly diverse group of economic entities, as the recent history of labor relations in the industry has proved, understanding them can be a difficult task. Generalizations can be made, however, about the similarities and differences among those economic entities, and these generalizations can be very helpful in understanding labor relations in the trucking industry. The most common, and often repeated, of these generalizations is that trucking firms singly and as a group lack the financial resources to withstand a strike of anything but short duration. Historically, this generalization has resulted in an imbalance of bargaining power that overwhelmingly favors the IBT.

Regular route carriers, unlike other types of carriers, are not simply in the trucking business. Their business is rather one of distribution, in which the terminal(s) are central. The terminal is the point where freight changes hands between local and over-the-road drivers who are often in the employ of the same firm, or between over-the-road drivers in the employ of different firms. Historically, that point of interface made regular route carriers highly vulnerable to secondary pressure from organized local and/or over-the-road employees who refused to handle "hot cargo," i.e., goods belonging to firms that are involved in a labor dispute.

The terminal network needed to handle less-than-truckload lot general freight requires a far larger capital investment than is necessary to function as a contract or special commodity carrier. In addition, the managerial and manpower requirements of terminal operation make regular route carrier operations more labor intensive and more expensive than those of other carriers. Thus, it is not surprising that rates for less-than-truckload lot freight are higher than rates for truckload lot freight, although this fact does not necessarily reflect the relative profitability of the two types of freight.

The relative cost and profitability of less than truckload lot and truckload lot freight is significant because most regular route carriers of general freight are engaged in the handling of both types. It is not uncommon for a trucking firm to hold both regular and irregular route operating authority, enabling it to operate in both general freight and special commodity markets. In such cases, a firm typically creates a special commodity division to handle its irregular route business. This type of structure avoids the traditional/contractual work practices in less-than-truckload lot operations that are not appropriate in truckload lot operations, most notably the division of labor between local and over-the-road operations and personnel. The IBT has contractually sanctioned such diversification by unionized regular route carriers through regional "special commodity riders." Such riders permit general freight firms to establish functionally and physically separate special commodity divisions to haul truckload lots of agreed-upon commodities directly from shipper to receiver. In addition, such riders permit those carriers to use owner-operators in moving such freight, provided that these owner-operators are or become members of the union and that the company makes full contributions for the owner-operators to the union's pension and health and welfare funds. The effect of the special commodity rider was to make the union a discriminating monopolist engaged in the practice of "maintaining a high price (wage) to those buyers who can afford it (general commodities), while charging a lower price to those who cannot (special commodities), for the same product (transportation service)." [22]

The special commodity rider originated in the Midwest in the early 1960s and initially applied only to iron and steel products. Over the following decade, it spread not only to other regions but expanded the definition of special commodities. The result was "a much more rapid rate of increase in the gross revenues from the special-commodities as compared to the general-commodities divisions of large carriers." [23] That pattern of revenue growth suggests that profit opportunities in special commodity freight were superior to those in general freight in the 1970s. One explanation for that phenomenon may be that the expanding list of special commodities enabled carriers to operate not only in the market for "commodity-rated" traffic, where rates were closely linked to marginal cost, but also in the market for "class-rated" traffic, where rates more closely approximated average or fully distributed costs, including those associated with general freight operations. [24]

The union's special commodity riders recognized and attempted to co-opt the growing role of owner-operators in the contract and irregular route special commodity segment of the intercity freight market. Owner-operators are individuals who own their own tractors but lack the ICC operating authority to serve as regulated carriers. Thus, to utilize their equipment, they must either act as exempt carriers or lease themselves to a regulated carrier. Historically, however, owner-operators have been forbidden by the ICC from leasing themselves directly to private carriers on the grounds that such arrangements constitute unauthorized contract carriage. Some owner-operators maintain membership in the Teamsters to facilitate leasing themselves to unionized carriers, but most do not because they see themselves as independent contractors rather than as employees.

A 1982 General Accounting Office report to the United States Congress indicated that in 1980 the yearly average number of self-employed truckers was 193,000. [25] That same report also indicated that "between 1972 and 1980, employment for Teamster general

---

[22] Levinson, "Trucking," p. 110.

[23] *Ibid.*, pp. 138-39.

[24] Irwin H. Silberman, "Statement Before the Subcommittee on Surface Transportation, Committee on Commerce, Science and Transportation, U.S. Senate," September 21, 1983, Washington, D.C., p. 12 (transcript in author's possession).

[25] U.S. General Accounting Office, "Effects of Regulatory Reform on Unemployment in the Trucking Industry," Report to the Honorable Dennis DeConcini, U.S. Senate (Gaithersburg, Md.: Government Printing Office, CED-82-90, June 11, 1982), p. 9.

freight carriers was virtually unchanged while the self-employed sector grew by 43 percent . . .," and concluded that one of the two major sources of "industry competition to Teamster general freight carriers has come from growing numbers of independent owner-operators."[26] In that context, it is interesting to note Garnel's historical characterization of owner-operators as

> highly unreliable [union] members. Their outlook was clearly that of small businessmen aspiring to become big businessmen. They might be organized through the use of coercion, but they reverted to non-union status as soon as coercive pressure was removed.[27]

---

[26] *Ibid.,* pp. 13 and 14.
[27] Donald Garnel, *The Rise of Teamster Power in the West* (Berkeley: University of California Press, 1972), p. 58.

CHAPTER III

The Regulation of the Trucking Industry

The basic framework of motor carrier regulation was established in the Motor Carrier Act (MCA) of 1935, and remained in place until passage of the MCA of 1980. The MCA of 1935 was but one manifestation of the general perception, fostered by the Great Depression, that "competition was 'destructive', that price structures were chaotic, and that market forces could not be relied upon to produce satisfactory results."[1] That perception, in turn, fostered a demand to protect industry from its destructive competitive instincts, spawning a set of New Deal policies designed to "restrict, eliminate, or modify the forces of competition,"[2] including the National Industrial Recovery Act (NIRA) of 1933 and its progeny, the MCA of 1935.

In the early 1930s the trucking industry seemed to provide a clear example of destructive competition. The industry, in the view of the American Trucking Associations (ATA), was "unstable and chaotic."[3] The chaos and instability in trucking were perceived to be the product of three forces: first, "any person with enough capital to buy a truck could enter the motor carrier business at will"; second, "owners, free to send their trucks wherever they wanted them to go, competed for the most lucrative routes . . . and ignored less profitable runs"; and third, "every operator set his own rates, usually just slightly above the breakeven point because of the cutthroat competition," enabling "trucking gypsies . . . [to] undercut the rates of established companies and upset the economics of the industry."[4]

The destructive competitive practices of trucking gypsies convinced established operators and firms that the industry's survival depended upon establishment of some restraint and order. Trucking

---

[1] Council on Wage and Price Stability, "A Report from the Council on Wage and Price Stability on the Value of Motor Carrier Operating Authorities," (Washington, D.C.: Council on Wage and Price Stability, June 9, 1977), p. 3.

[2] *Ibid.*

[3] Gary M. LaBella, *A Glance Back* (Washington, D.C.: American Trucking Associations, 1977), p. 18.

[4] *Ibid.*

operators and firms joined with the railroads, whose markets were being eroded by trucking, and the railroad unions, whose jobs were being lost to truckers, in demanding that the government regulate motor freight transport. These demands finally were met with the passage of the MCA of 1935, which granted the Interstate Commerce Commission (ICC) regulatory authority over the trucking industry.

Regulation of motor carriers was expected to serve the public interest by "placing motor carriers on a regulatory par with railroads,"[5] and the industry's private interest was to be served by stabilization of prices and capacity. The ICC, in serving those interests, adapted its techniques of railroad regulation, originally designed to control monopoly, to the control of competition in the trucking and freight industries.

THE MOTOR CARRIER ACT

The MCA of 1935 was an extension of the Interstate Commerce Act, which was passed in 1887 to regulate the railroads.[6] The 1887 legislation, originally entitled the Act to Regulate Commerce, was intended to control the natural monopolies railroads possessed on some routes through regulation of rates and routes. The MCA placed interstate trucking under the same regulatory agency, subject to the following congressional mandate stated in section 202(a) of the act:

> It is hereby declared to be the policy of Congress to regulate transportation by motor carriers in such manner as to recognize and preserve the inherent advantages of, and foster sound economic conditions in, such transportation and among such carriers in the public interest; promote adequate, economical, and efficient service by motor carriers, and reasonable charges therefor, without unjust discrimination, undue preferences or advantages, and unfair or destructive competitive practices.[7]

To enable the ICC to fulfill its mandate, Congress granted the agency broad authority to control entry into the interstate trucking market, the extent of operation within the market, and rates charged in the market. Such control permitted the ICC to determine the number of carriers that could operate in any area, to define what products carriers could haul and where and over what routes they could haul them, and to decide the rates that carriers could charge. In addition, the agency was empowered to set requirements for vehicle safety,

---

[5] Council on Wage and Price Stability, "A Report from the Council," p. 3.
[6] 24 Stat. 379.
[7] Motor Carrier Act of 1935, chapter 498, 49 Stat. 543, section 202a.

employee hours, and cargo insurance. (This last set of responsibilies was transferred to the newly formed Department of Transportation in the mid-1960s.)

Control of Entry

The ICC's control of entry into the industry rested in the statute requiring regulated for-hire carriers to receive operating authority from the commission. If a carrier could demonstrate that it had performed the service described in its application for operating authority prior to passage of the MCA, it was entitled to such authority without a hearing under a so-called grandfather clause. Carriers seeking new (or extended) routes or rights had to justify the public need for their service in a hearing before the commission, and any existing carrier serving the market in question could contest that need. On the basis of such a hearing, the ICC could grant, in whole or part, or deny a request for new operating authority.

Upon successful application for operating authority, a common carrier would receive a "certificate of public convenience and necessity."[8] Section 207(a) of the act specified the conditions under which such a certificate was to be granted:

> a certificate shall be issued to any qualified application therefor, authorizing the whole or any part of the operations covered by the application, if it is found that the applicant is fit, willing, and able properly to perform the service proposed and to conform to the provisions of this part and the requirements, rules, and regulations of the Commission thereunder, and that the proposed service, to the extent to be authorized by the certificate, is or will be required by the present or future public convenience and necessity; otherwise such application shall be denied.[9]

A successful applicant for private contract operating authority would be issued a permit. Section 209(b) of the act set forth that

> a permit shall be issued to any qualified applicant therefor, authorizing in whole or part the operations covered by the application, if it appears from the applications or from any hearing held thereon, that the applicant is fit, willing, and able properly to perform the service of a contract carrier by motor vehicle, and to conform to the provisions of this part and the lawful requirements, rules, and regulations of the Commission thereunder, and that the proposed operation, to the extent authorized by the permit, will be consistent with the public interest . . . otherwise such application shall be denied.[10]

---

[8] *Ibid.*, section 207a.
[9] *Ibid.*
[10] *Ibid.*, section 209b.

Control of Operations

The ICC's regulatory authority and responsibility extended beyond control of entry to control of both the structure and scope of
operation of authorized carriers. The statute required that the commission, in issuing certificates and permits, specify the nature and
extent of authorized service by individual carriers. In the case of
common carriers, section 208(a) of the act stipulated that:

> Any certificate issues . . . shall specify the service to be rendered and
> the routes over which, the fixed termini, if any, between which and
> the intermediate and off route points, if any, at which and in case of
> operations not over specified routes or between fixed termini, the
> territory within which the motor carrier is authorized to operate.[11]

In the case of contract carriers, section 209(b) of the act simply
required that "the Commission shall specify in the permit the business of the contract carrier covered and the scope thereof."[12] In
addition, it stipulated that the commission attach to the permit "at
the time of issuance, and from time to time thereafter, such reasonable terms, conditions, and limitations consistent with the character of the holder as a contract carrier as are necessary to carry
out . . . the requirements established by the Commission."[13]

Control of Rates

The MCA also gave the ICC a measure of control over rates and
ratemaking. Regulated for-hire carriers were required to publish
and maintain their rates for public inspection, and were prohibited
both from charging or collecting any tariff other than that published, and from offering rebates or discounts. Changes in published
rates had to be filed with the commission, which was empowered
to suspend any proposed rate change for up to 180 days upon com-
plaint of another carrier. The commission could also set maximum
and minimum rates for common carriers and minimum rates for
contract carriers if it deemed such action necessary.

IMPLEMENTATION OF THE ACT

The MCA of 1935 and its subsequent amendments and extensions
prior to 1980 gave the ICC relatively broad discretion in shaping
the operating structure of the interstate trucking industry. For four

---

[11] *Ibid.*, section 208a.
[12] *Ibid.*, 209b.
[13] *Ibid.*

decades, the ICC used its discretion to envelop the industry in a blanket of protective regulation in accordance with its mandate to discourage "unfair or destructive competitive practices." Yet at the same time, in the view of many observers, the ICC's practices ignored its mandate to "promote adequate, economical, and efficient service by motor carriers and reasonable charges therefor."[14] The result, according to a 1977 report by the Council on Wage and Price Stability, was a combination of higher rates and lower efficiency in the movement of freight by motor carrier. The council estimated that by the mid-1970s the cost to the economy was perhaps as much as $4 billion per year in trucking expenses.[15]

Control of Entry

The ICC quickly took its 1935 congressional mandate to discourage so-called destructive competition in the exercise of its licensing authority to heart. Shortly after passage of the act, the commission took the position that the phrase "public convenience and necessity," with respect to new operating authority, was a question of

> whether the new operation or service will serve a useful public purpose, responsive to public demand or need; whether this purpose can and will be served as well by existing lines or carriers; and whether it can be served by applicant with the operation or service proposed without endangering or impairing the operation of existing carriers contrary to the public interest.[16]

Consideration of the extent to which new entrants could endanger or impair existing operators constituted a potentially powerful device for restricting entry into the industry. The legitimacy of the device, and of a regulatory policy based on the prevention of injury as a result of competition, was at least indirectly recognized by the Supreme Court, which in a 1944 decision stated:

> The premises of motor carrier regulation posit some curtailment of free and unrestrained competition. The origins and legislative history of the Motor Carrier Act adequately disclose that in it Congress recognized that there may be occasions when competition between carriers may result in harm to the public as well as benefit; and that when a [carrier] inflicts injury upon its rival, it may be the public which ultimately bears the loss.[17]

The fact that the majority of operating rights in existence in the mid-1970s arose under the grandfather clause of the Motor Carrier

---

[14] *Ibid.*, 202a.
[15] Council on Wage and Price Stability, "A Report from the Council," p. 6.
[16] Pan-American Bus Lines Operation, 1 MCC 170 (1936).
[17] McLean Trucking Co. v. U.S., 321 U.S. 67, 83-88 (1944), 83-84.

Act clearly suggests that, under the MCA of 1935, the ICC pursued a policy based on the prevention of injury by competition in exercising its control of entry.[18] In 1977, the Council on Wage and Price Stability characterized the commission's policy as follows:

> The Commission may deny an application if it threatens the financial health of an existing carrier. As the ICC interprets the law, the owner of an authority is not protected from competition; he is, however, protected from so-called "destructive competition." This, in effect, means that it is exceedingly unlikely that a new entrant would be permitted if that entry would drive the existing carrier out of business or lead to substantial "harm." Thus, the operating authority protects individual firms who may successfully protest a threat to their existence. That is, the survival of individual firms is supported by regulatory policy, thereby reducing the risk of default associated with a normally competitive industry.[19]

The protective nature of regulatory policy made operating authority a valuable privilege; it constituted a license to operate a business without the degree of risk encountered in a competitive industry, and with a better-than-average opportunity to grow with the economy. As a result, an active market for existing operating authorities developed, and such authorities came to represent the industry's "most important asset"—an asset that, in the words of the ATA, "without regulation . . . would be totally worthless."[20] The value of, and market for, operating authority in the 1970s was supported by the fact that "virtually the only way [for a carrier to expand] was to buy additional rights through other motor carriers."[21]

Control of Operations

The protection afforded to established carriers by the ICC was not entirely without cost. The commission did not hesitate to exercise its regulatory authority to impose "terms, conditions, and limitations" on its grants of operating authority.[22] The result was a complex web of operating restrictions that impeded efficient trucking service.

A 1945 congressional study on the implementation of the MCA uncovered widespread commodity limitations on operating author-

---

[18] Council on Wage and Price Stability, "A Report from the Council," p. 8, n. 1.
[19] *Ibid.*, p. 8.
[20] *Transport Topics*, July 19, 1976, p. 14.
[21] Peter T. Beardsley, Vice-President and General Counsel for the ATA, letter to the ICC, seeking the ICC's support before the Financial Accounting Standards Board, July 14, 1972.
[22] Motor Carrier Act of 1935, chapter 498, 49 Stat. 543, section 209b.

ity.[23] Sixty-two percent of intercity freight certificates, the study found, had been limited to special commodities. Among haulers subject to such limitations, only 8 percent required special equipment that prevented them from handling other commodities. Two-thirds of the remaining carriers were limited to three or fewer special commodities or commodity groups and 40 percent were limited to one commodity or commodity class. Thirty-two percent of intercity carriers held general commodity authority, subject to numerous exceptions.

The study also found significant limitations on the ability of carriers to secure balanced loads, which are an important element in efficient trucking service.[24] Over one-third of intercity carriers were limited in some manner from obtaining income-generating backhauls. One-tenth were entirely prohibited from taking return loads for compensation. Private carriers were prohibited from soliciting backhaul freight on a for-hire basis, which generally forced them to return empty to their point of origin.

Finally, the study uncovered a complex set of route restrictions that forced carriers to travel unnecessary distances, often partially or totally empty.[25] Only 30 percent of regular route carriers had full authority to serve all intermediate points along their routes; 10 percent had no such authority. Only 8 percent of irregular route carriers held authority to offer service between all points in their areas. In addition, so-called gateway restrictions, applied to irregular route traffic, required that movements between areas previously served and those served as a result of new authority be through points common to both areas.

The obvious solution to many of the efficiency problems created by these restrictions was extension of operating authority to fill the gaps in a firm's system. Established firms pursued this option during the first decade of regulation, but apparently with little success. The 1945 congressional study cited earlier found that

> the Commission is disposed to reject every extension of operating authority calculated to improve the efficiency of the applicant's operations if the extension would increase the competition for any traffic for which inadequate service has not been demonstrated.[26]

---

[23] Board of Investigation and Research, *Federal Regulatory Restrictions upon Motor and Water Carriers*, Senate Document No. 78, 79th Congress, 1st Session, 1945, pp. 27-36.
[24] *Ibid.*, pp. 76-80.
[25] *Ibid.*, pp. 96-116.
[26] *Ibid.*, pp. 118-19.

The web of ICC control over operation was equally complex, if slightly less burdensome, in 1975. The Council on Wage and Price Stability characterized the situation in the mid-1970s as follows:

> Certificates contain various restrictions including, among others, specification of routes, gateway restrictions, limitations to haul goods in one direction only, and restrictions as to particular commodities hauled. Some of the inefficiencies in route and service offerings have been mitigated by both the Commission and the carriers themselves as larger firms have purchased complementary authorities from smaller firms. The problem, however, is far from resolved. Many carrier route structures remain circuitous and route and service offerings remain quite inflexible to changes in demand.[27]

Efficiency considerations had clearly become an important factor in supporting the market for, and market value of, operating authorities by the mid-1970s. In that context, they were a major force favoring consolidation and concentration in the regulated segment of the industry. In the late 1970s, the 100 largest of the 17,000 firms in that segment of the industry accounted for approximately 30 percent of the total operating revenues of regulated motor carriers.[28]

Control of Rates

The ICC's greatest regulatory challenge came in the control of rates. The trucking industry, in marked contrast to the railroads, was a diverse, atomistic, and competitive industry with a staggering array of potential routes and rates. To simplify its task in regulating what could have been an unmanageably large and complex set of freight rates, the ICC encouraged regulated carriers to engage in joint ratemaking through the vehicle of rate bureaus.

In 1980, ten major general freight rate bureaus were operating in different sections of the country to assist carriers in setting their rates and justifying them to the ICC. In addition, approximately fifty-five smaller bureaus offered ratemaking service and assistance to local or special commodity carriers, assisted in this task by the National Motor Freight Traffic Association, which is essentially a national forum in which carriers and shippers discuss and establish the commodity classifications to which individual rates apply.

The activities of these rate bureaus have since their inception clearly constituted and involved price fixing, an illegal activity under the nation's antitrust laws. That legal conflict was not resolved until 1948, when Congress passed the Reed-Bullwinkle Act, which provided that the activities of rate bureaus were to be exempt from

---

[27] Council on Wage and Price Stability, "A Report from the Council," pp. 4-5.

[28] U.S. Department of Commerce, *The Biennial Supplement to the Survey of Current Business, 1979* (Washington, D.C.: Government Printing Office, N.D.), p. 108.

antitrust laws as long as their bylaws and procedures were approved by the commission, and under the condition that the right of independent ratemaking was protected.[29]

The ratemaking structure of the industry and the commission since 1948 preserved the legal, if not necessarily the practical, right of individual ratemaking. Individual rate actions are subject to both protest by other carriers and suspension by the ICC for up to 180 days. If a rate is protested and suspended, the burden of proof is on the proposing carrier to show that its proposed rate is just, reasonable, and, specifically, compensatory. That burden and its attendant delay and litigation costs constitute a formidable deterrent to individual ratemaking; an analysis of motor freight bills done in the late 1970s revealed that less than 3 percent of all general freight and 9 percent of all less-than-truckload freight shipments moved under independently filed rates.[30]

The Council on Wage and Price Stability concluded in 1977 that regulation had virtually extinguished independent ratemaking because such action "is easily challenged at the Interstate Commerce Commission and easily discouraged by the motor carrier rate bureau."[31] In that context, the council characterized the industry's pricing system in the following terms:

> The ratemaking mechanism thus reflects the combined effects of concerted carrier action which is immune to the anti-trust laws and the judgment of the ICC as to what constitutes a fair return for groups of carriers taken as a whole. The result has been inflexible prices and the virtual elimination of intra-modal price competition.[32]

The elimination of intramodal price competition forces firms to compete for business on a service basis. Regulatory restrictions on operations may impede such competition, thereby creating both a service and a cost incentive to circumvent such restrictions by acquiring additional authority. At the same time, however, as the costs of service are reflected in price, a growing potential market may emerge for no-frills service—a phenomenon that may account, in part, for the rapid expansion of private carriage in the 1970s, despite the pervasive problem of empty backhauls.[33]

---

[29] James C. Johnson and James P. Rakowski, "The Reed-Bullwinkle Act (1948): A Thirty Year Perspective," *Transportation Research Forum Proceedings—Nineteenth Annual Meeting, 1978*, Volume 19, No. 1.

[30] U.S. House of Representatives, Ninety-Sixth Congress, Hearings Before the Subcommittee on Surface Transportation of the Committee on Public Works and Transportation, First Session, Part 1, pp. 292-97.

[31] Council on Wage and Price Stability, "A Report from the Council," p. 4.

[32] *Ibid.*, p. 4.

[33] *Ibid.*, p. 30.

CONSEQUENCES OF REGULATION FOR THE
ORGANIZATION OF LABOR

The fundamental effect of regulation was to transform intercity for-hire motor freight cartage from a highly competitive to a highly cartelized industry. The cartelization of the industry did not totally eliminate competition, but did change its focus from price to service in such forms as more frequent schedules (often leading to partial loads or empty backhauls), overnight delivery, and other services. In the view of the Council on Wage and Price Stability,

> one effect of this type of "cartelized" competition is to raise costs, increase operating ratios, and reduce returns thus sanctioning existing high rates as well as providing a basis for the justification of further rate increases.[34]

Historically, the costs of service competition were not closely scrutinized or controlled by the ICC in its rate-regulating activity. Thus, although those costs tended to reduce possible monopoly profits, they did not prevent regulated carriers from realizing a substantial and possibly excessive (given regulatory protection against risk of competitive injury) return on investment. In the early 1970s, after-tax return on investment for Class I motor carriers ranged from 9 to 17 percent, a range that "is in excess of that earned by public utilities and compares favorably with private return in unregulated markets."[35]

The cartelization of the industry under regulation benefited a second interested party—the International Brotherhood of Teamsters. Its fundamental institutional challenge as a union is to organize to the extent of the market and to standardize wages. Regulation and cartelization greatly simplified its task, as trucking grew from a $1 billion industry in 1940 to a $20 billion industry in 1975, and thus the Teamsters shared in the economic benefits of cartelization. An unpublished study cited by the Council on Wage and Price Stability reports that the annual earnings differential between drivers and their helpers and all other workers in manufacturing increased from 19 percent in 1938 to 76 percent in 1972.[36] This fact prompted the council to conclude that "freight rates have provided an excessive return to trucking firms and very hefty increases in wages for drivers and helpers."[37]

---

[34] *Ibid.*
[35] *Ibid.*, p. 13.
[36] *Ibid.*, p. 31.
[37] *Ibid.*

Entry

The postwar growth in value and volume of regulated trucking, which occured with no corresponding growth in the number of regulated truckers, dramatically demonstrated the effects of the ICC's policies regarding entry into the industry. Between 1950 and 1975, the value of freight moved by regulated motor carriers increased six-fold, and the volume of such freight increased three-fold. Over the same period the number of regulated carriers actually declined by about 20 percent, from 19,597 to 16,005.[38]

The decline in the total number of regulated carriers does not mean that there were no new entrants to the industry during the period, but it does suggest that most of the industry's growth over the period was experienced by a limited and stable population of established carriers whose operations were expanding by virtue of growing demand on existing routes and/or added demand on new routes authorized by the ICC or acquired from other carriers. Established carriers thus inevitably presented a visible and accessible organizing target for the Teamsters.

The net attrition in regulated carriers from more than 21,000 in 1946 to a low of 15,000 in 1970 significantly reduced the Teamster's task in securing and maintaining its organizational hold on the industry. The IBT's organizing effort was aided by ICC policies, which by the mid-1950s were acknowledged to "have been a prime factor in discouraging and pressing small carriers from regulated trucking and in encouraging the growth of the larger carriers."[39] Some thirty years later, the ICC's role in sustaining the Teamsters' hold on the industry was stated as follows:

> In naturally competitive industries regulation may strengthen organized labor by making nonunionized competition less effective. [Trucking] regulation prevents new nonunionized firms from entering the industry and competing for the traffic carried by the unionized firms.[40]

It is impossible to determine exactly the extent to which the ICC's "no injury" policy, as applied both at point of entry and in individual ratemaking, deterred entry by nonunion firms, or made newly established firms less effective competitors. It seems unlikely that the

---

[38] American Trucking Associations, Inc., *American Trucking Trends 1979-1980* (Washington, D.C.: ATA, Inc.), pp. 21, 35, 38.

[39] Hearings Before the Select Committee on Small Business, U.S. Senate, *ICC Administration of the Motor Carrier Act*, 84th Congress, 1st Session, 1955, p. 246.

[40] Thomas G. Moore, "The Beneficiaries of Trucking Regulation," *Journal of Law and Economics*, Vol. XXI, No. 2, (October 1978), pp. 331-32.

policy had no significant effect, however. The absence of both existing and prospective nonunion competition lowers the potential competitive cost of agreeing to higher wages, although not necessarily the economic cost of doing so; thus, in practice, the regulatory statutes, as interpreted by the ICC, simplified union organization of the industry and standardization of its wages.

Operations

The complex web of restrictions and limitations on operating authorities had its own economic and institutional impact on the industry. The ICC's policy of prohibiting private carriers from soliciting backhaul freight on a for-hire basis served to slow the growth of private carriage as a potential no-frills competitor to existing trucking operations, and the ICC's practice of limiting the number of shippers a contract carrier can serve—the so-called rule of eight—did the same for contract carriage. Route and commodity restrictions likewise curtailed competitive growth for both types of carriers. As a result, freight rates reflected, among other factors, "the inefficiencies of constrained competition and the inflexibility of route structures."[41]

The inefficiencies and inflexibilities imposed on the industry by regulation required excess capacity in the industry. The excess capacity involved both equipment and employment, and served to support a relatively high and fairly stable demand for both capital and labor. This created an economic environment favorable to the IBT in its efforts to organize and represent workers. The same inefficiencies and inflexibilities also aided the union institutionally, since constrained competition and market segmentation reduced the amount of organizing effort necessary to cover the market or markets. Route restrictions forced carriers to create centrally located cargo depots, which could and did serve as key pressure points in the union's efforts to extend and defend its institutional presence in the industry.

Rates

In a regulated industry, incentive to achieve efficiency may be severely weakened. In such cases, management may elect to achieve its allowed rate of return by following the path of least resistance. That path may lead management to "avoid or minimize confron-

---

[41] Council on Wage and Price Stability, "A Report from the Council," p. 31.

tations with labor as well as the stern cost-cutting measures one frequently finds in unregulated industries."[42]

The trucking industry was heavily unionized, and therefore, workers' wages were negotiated rather than set in a competitive market. The market forces that tend to check the rise of negotiated input prices in nonregulated industries are weakened in regulated industries if higher negotiated input prices can be passed on to consumers with little or no loss of business. The trucking industry under regulation fit that model fairly well in that returns to capital (not rates or costs) were regulated, entry was restricted and protection the rule, import and intermodal competition posed little threat, and rates were set on a concerted basis.[43]

In such a situation, "if the return to capital is rigorously regulated by the Commission, the gain from excessive prices may accrue to those factors of production whose prices are not regulated."[44] That possibility seemed likely in the trucking industry given the character of the industry, its constituent firms, and its dominant union. Specifically, it has been argued that

> (1) since the industry is comprised, in the main, of small firms dealing in a service, a disproportionate share of bargaining power belongs to the union. As a result, the final wage settlement lies close to the management's maximum acceptable level. (2) ICC regulation of price and entry have increased the employers ability to pay. (3) Hence, the excess profits of the cartel have been expropriated by the IBT and divided among its members.[45]

This view explains how regulation provided the "hefty increases in wages for drivers and helpers" previously noted. It contradicts, however, the fact that regulation also provided "excessive returns to trucking firms."[46] The resolution of that seeming paradox rests in the way in which the ICC exercises its rate regulation authority:

> The ICC bases its rate regulation on the average operating ratio . . . defined as the ratio of operating costs to total revenue. Thus, an increase in Teamster wages usually triggers ICC approval of a rate increase. Since over 60 percent of operating costs are labor expend-

---

[42] Milton Kafoglis, "Before the Interstate Commerce Commission Investigation and Suspension Docket No. M-29772 General Increase, S.M.C.R.C. April, 1978 Verified Statement of Milton Kafoglis," (Washington, D.C.: Council on Wage and Price Stability, July 5, 1978), p. 2.

[43] *Ibid.*, p. 7.

[44] *Ibid.*

[45] James E. Annable, Jr., "The ICC, the IBT and the Cartelization of the American Trucking Industry," *Quarterly Review of Economics and Business*, Vol. 13, No. 2 (Summer 1973), p. 40.

[46] Council on Wage and Price Stability, "A Report from the Council," p. 31.

itures ... more labor or higher wages for the industry as a whole may actually increase total [absolute] profits.[47]

Recent evidence indicates that regulation may bias wage settlements in an upward direction. An analysis of average hourly earnings data for the 1970-1977 period by the Council on Wage and Price Stability revealed an 86.8 percent increase over the period in regulated industries (including trucking), as compared with 76.1 percent in highly unionized manufacturing and mining and 67.7 percent for all manufacturing.[48] That bias, however, was less apparent in trucking, which experienced an 81.1 percent increase, than in railroads (Class I), which experienced a 90.0 percent increase, or intercity highway transit, which experienced an 82.6 percent increase.[49] Nonetheless, trucking employees fared well vis-à-vis their counterparts in highly unionized manufacturing and mining.

---

[46] Moore, p. 332.
[48] Kafoglis, Table 1.
[49] *Ibid.*, Table 3.

CHAPTER IV

The Organization of the Industry

The evolution and economics of intercity trucking from 1940 to 1980 were shaped by two basic institutional forces. The first was government regulation through the Interstate Commerce Commission (ICC). The second, and almost as powerful, was collective bargaining and the International Brotherhood of Teamsters (IBT or Teamsters). In the mid-1970s the IBT had an estimated 400,000 members in its freight division,[1] of which perhaps 75 percent were covered under its most visible mechanism of control over the industry: the National Master Freight Agreement (NMFA).

The IBT is a large, powerful, and diverse union that has made its organizational presence felt well beyond the limits of the craft jurisdiction to which it adhered through much of its history. The IBT claimed a membership of 1.6 million in 1983, making it the nation's largest union.[2] Of that number, only one-fifth were in its freight division, with only about one-quarter of those engaged in the intercity movement of freight. Yet the crucial role of its freight division members in the movement of goods has given the union a measure of power and organization appeal above and beyond their number. The IBT, after its departure from the AFL-CIO in 1957, actively exploited its appeal and became a union without jurisdictional boundaries. This situation was in marked contrast to the Teamsters' homogeneous character in the late 1940s, when one prescient observer noted:

> Because of the great striking power of the Teamsters, it possesses an organizing potential that has scarcely been tapped. All kinds of workers have from time to time sought admission into this powerful union, thus far without success because of self-imposed jurisdictional limitations. ... If, as there is reason to suspect, the Teamsters should

---

[1] Harold M. Levinson, "Trucking," in *Collective Bargaining: Contemporary American Experience*, ed. Gerald G. Somers (Madison, Wis.: Industrial Relations Research Association, 1982), pp. 103-4.

[2] Leo Troy and Neil Sheflin, *U.S. Union Sourcebook* (West Orange, N.J.: Industrial Relations Data and Information Services, 1985), pp. 3-16.

decide to let down the bars ... the repercussions will be something to observe.[3]

The IBT's members are organized in about 750 locals, which in turn are organized in 48 joint councils and 5 area conferences— Western, Southern, Central, Eastern, and Canadian.[4] Joint councils were first created in 1904, when the union's constitution was amended to create such councils in any city where two or more locals in different industry classifications existed. Area conferences evolved out of the union's efforts to organize over-the-road drivers between 1935 and 1955, and they were given full recognition and support in 1961, when the union's constitution was amended to require that

> all Local Unions and Joint Councils must affiliate with, and partic-ipate in the activities of the Area Conference and State and Multi-State Conferences, if any, having geographic or awarded jurisdiction over such Local Union and Joint Council.[5]

The formal governmental structure of the IBT is like that of most unions. Ultimate authority rests with the union convention, which meets every five years. Between conventions, the affairs of the union are under the direction of its general president, general secretary, and general executive board, all of which are elected by the convention.

In its direction of union affairs, the elected leadership of the IBT over the past three decades has been far from exemplary in its performance. The fact that the union has been anything but a model of democracy and honesty in its operation has embroiled it and its leadership in a seemingly endless stream of legal battles with the federal government, and has also produced at least the seeds of internal revolt in the form of a small but highly visible and vocal dissident group called Teamsters for a Democratic Union (TDU).

The fundamental goal of the IBT in the trucking industry has been to take labor out of competition by organizing to the extent of the market and standardizing labor costs. Historically, this has not been an easy task, given the fragmentation and diversity that characterize the industry in terms of both management and labor. The task was somewhat simplified by the advent of government regulation and support of collective bargaining in the mid-1930s, but the solution to the problem was ultimately left to the ingenuity

---

[3] Nathan P. Feinsinger, *Collective Bargaining in the Trucking Industry* (Philadel-phia: University of Pennsylvania Press, 1949), pp. 23-24.

[4] Levinson, "Trucking," p. 103, n. 10.

[5] International Brotherhood of Teamsters, *Proceedings, Eighteenth Convention* (Miami Beach, Fla., July 3-7, 1961), p. 603.

of the IBT, which produced two leaders more than equal to that challenge—Dave Beck and Jimmy Hoffa. Their response to the challenge might best be termed ruthless and pragmatic unionism— ruthless in dealing with their enemies, and pragmatic in dealing with their friends.

THE DRIVE TO UNIONIZE

The roots of organization in the trucking industry can be traced to the formation of local drayage associations, in the East during the colonial period and in the West in the 1850s. Such associations functioned more as guilds of owner-operators concerned with dray- age rates than as unions of drivers concerned with wages, a dis- tinction that became increasingly evident with the growth of drayage firms during the nineteenth century. As the distinction became manifest, some existing associations evolved into local em- ployer associations, and others became local driver unions.[6]

The first national union in the industry, the Team Drivers' In- ternational Union, was formed in 1898 and was chartered by the AFL in 1899.[7] Membership was open to owner-drivers with six or fewer teams as well as to employee drivers. The majority of its initial 1,200 members was apparently composed of owner-drivers, and as a result its early efforts produced increases in drayage rates but not increases in wages for hired drivers. The emphasis on ac- tivities designed to benefit owners exclusively prompted the for- mation in 1902 of a rival organization, the Teamsters National Union of America, which barred from membership owners with hired employees.

The AFL merged the two organizations in 1903 to form what would become the International Brotherhood of Teamsters, which had a total combined membership of approximately 32,000.[8] Two years later, a number of its local unions, including the Chicago local that had been instrumental in the formation of the Teamsters Na- tional Union, withdrew and formed another rival organization, the United Teamsters of America. That organization disintegrated in 1908, when most of the dissident locals returned to the fold. The Teamsters and Helpers Union of Chicago did not rejoin the IBT, however, and remained independent until 1934.[9]

---

[6] Donald Garnel, *The Rise of Teamster Power in the West* (Berkeley: University of California Press, 1972).

[7] *Ibid.*, p. 34.

[8] Ralph C. James and Estelle Dinerstein James, *Hoffa and the Teamsters: A Study of Union Power* (Princeton: D. Van Nostrand Company, 1965), p. 14.

[9] Garnel, *Rise of Teamster Power*, p. 37.

When it was formed in 1903, the jurisdiction of the IBT was defined as drivers and helpers of horsedrawn wagons. Not until 1910 did the union's jurisdiction formally extend to motor carriage, and at that time its name was changed to the International Brotherhood of Teamsters, Chauffeurs, Warehousemen and Helpers of America. The union extended its jurisdiction to its present "all workers—without limitation" in 1961, following its expulsion from the AFL-CIO because of racketeering infiltration.

The Extent of Organization

The organizational task confronting the IBT in 1903 was strictly local, since the industry in which it operated was confined to local delivery. The narrow scope of the union's early organizational task fostered a fairly narrow focus on so-called delivery crafts, such as coal, ice, milk, and bread delivery, and permitted a high degree of local autonomy within the union in the organization and representation of those crafts.

The union proved highly erratic in meeting its local organizational challenges. In a number of major cities in the East and Midwest (New York, Detroit, Chicago, St. Louis) it was highly successful, while in other cities and in smaller communities it was not. Where successful, its organizing efforts all too often took the form of top-down organizing, which was characterized by collusion and crime as the basis for employer recognition in exchange for union enforcement of uniform terms and conditions. One such collusive arrangement was reached in the San Francisco Bay area, an early western center of Teamster power, where the IBT gained a union shop and wage increases in exchange for the promise that its members would work only for members of the Draymen's Association and proprietary carriers who paid union wages, and that it would undertake to see that all draymen joined the association.[10]

The emergence of over-the-road trucking in the 1920s altered the strictly local character of the industry, but only to the extent that over-the-road drivers constituted a competitive threat to local drivers in the local delivery of goods. That threat apparently remained sufficiently limited throughout the 1920s that local unions saw no need to organize over-the-road carriers or their drivers. Most locals continued to focus attention on the delivery crafts, and ignored the organizational potential of intercity motor carriers until well into the 1930s. The attitude of local unions was reflected in the view of

---

[10] *Ibid.*, p. 48.

the union president that highway drivers were unworthy "trash" in comparison to local delivery craftsmen.[11]

The indifference of most local unions and the international union to the organizing frontier of over-the-road trucking was challenged by two union officials—Dave Beck on the West Coast (Seattle), and in the Midwest, Farrell Dobbs (Minneapolis), who was eventually succeeded by Jimmy Hoffa (Detroit). Dobbs' perception of the need to organize over-the-road drivers was economically based, since he believed that "miserable working conditions among any group of drivers is a potential threat to better working conditions among other drivers."[12] Beck's perception of the need to organize over-the-road drivers was also institutionally based, since he saw in such organization the "opportunity to organize not only Los Angeles, but all of the little towns and cities," with the result that "a tremendous number of local cartage workers . . . were organized because they were feeders to the long-line haulers, and dependent upon them."[13] Hoffa, like Beck, perceived that "once you have the road men, you can get the local cartage, and once you have the local cartage, you can get anyone you want."[14]

The strategic goal of both Beck and Dobbs was to build upon the union's existing local base to organize over-the-road trucking on an area basis, and then to build on that area base to extend organization to a regional basis. Beck sought to implement that strategy from his base in Seattle by increasing coordination of the activities of joint councils, first on a statewide basis, and then on a regional basis. The result was the formation of a Western Conference in 1937. In the same year, Dobbs formed the Central States Drivers Conference "to promote the organization of workers engaged in transportation throughout the entire district and to establish uniform wages, hours and working conditions."[15] That district, as originally constituted, encompassed thirteen locals in six states, but was expanded one year later to forty-six locals in eleven states. Neither Beck nor Dobbs succeeded by 1940 in completing the organization of the industry on a regional basis, but their combined efforts established an institutional foundation for such organization. The task of strengthening and perfecting that basis was left to Dave Beck and Jimmy Hoffa, first as regional and later as national leaders of the union.

---

[11] James and James, *Hoffa and the Teamsters*, pp. 91-92.
[12] *Ibid.*, p. 91, quoting statements in the *Northwest Organizer*, May 26, 1938, p. 3.
[13] Garnel, *Rise of Teamster Power*, p. 103.
[14] James and James, *Hoffa and the Teamsters*, p. 100.
[15] *Ibid.*, p. 92.

The Extension of Organization

The efforts of Beck and Dobbs to organize over-the-road drivers in the West and Midwest in the 1930s coincided with and benefitted from the emergence of public policies that supported unionism and collective bargaining. The National Industrial Recovery Act (NIRA), passed in 1933, explicitly recognized the right of workers to organize, and implicitly encouraged them to do so. As a result, "thousands of drivers, especially the employees of larger carriers, voluntarily joined the union all over the country."[16] Far more important for the success of Teamster efforts, however, was the passage of the Norris-LaGuardia Act in 1932, which lifted judicial restraints on strikes, picketing, and boycotts and opened the way for the union to use its economic muscle to gain bargaining rights for thousands of other drivers with or without their active consent.

The union's approach to organizing over-the-road trucking was the same top-down method utilized in the organization of local cartage; the union exercised its power to impede the movement of freight in areas where it was strong in order to compel recognition in areas where it was weak. The key tactical element in this organizing strategy was the secondary work boycott—the refusal of union members to handle cargo carried by nonunion drivers. The key point of confrontation between union and nonunion drivers was the terminal, where intercity cargo was tendered, assembled or disassembled, and delivered by organized local cartage carriers. Terminals also served as transfer points for interlined freight between carriers who lacked the requisite operating authority to handle freight from origin to destination.

Secondary boycotts put pressure on shippers to avoid use of nonunion carriers. Such carriers, faced with a loss of business, could ill afford to resist recognition of the union, particularly when it faced competition over its major routes. In this context, regular route common carriers were the most vulnerable, but irregular route and contract carriers were not invulnerable, given the willingness and ability of the union to carry its case to the loading docks of organized shippers and organized recipients of goods.

The passage of the Wagner Act in 1935 introduced the principles of employee self-determination and free choice into national labor policy. It did not foresee the need to protect the right of free choice against interference by unions, however, and did little to induce

---

[16] Garnel, *Rise of Teamster Power*, p. 114.

the Teamsters to abandon its traditional organizing techniques. As Millis and Brown note:

> Some unions were so powerful that they could and sometimes did coerce employers, especially small employers, and their employees, by [show or threat of economic power] rather than following the democratic process of organizing people and proving their right to recognition as majority representative. This was an especially serious problem in some areas, . . . and with some unions, as the Teamsters.[17]

The IBT's organizing techniques, despite being at odds with the spirit of the law, proved highly effective. The union's membership grew from an estimated 75,000 in 1933 to 420,000 by 1939, and to 920,000 by 1948.[18] The extent of the union's presence in intercity trucking grew as dramatically as its membership, from virtually no organization in 1933 to an estimated 50 percent of intercity trucking under contract by the end of the 1930s,[19] increasing to an estimated 80 percent under contract by the end of World War II.[20]

The organizational challenge facing the union in the 1950s was to maintain and consolidate its presence in areas in which it was still weak, primarily the South. In meeting that challenge, the union was aided by the ICC, the regulatory policies of which produced a declining population of regulated carriers and a growing number of large interregional and interdependent carriers. Such carriers would have been relatively easy targets for organization by traditional coercive means, had the Taft-Hartley Act not specifically sought to outlaw such means, particularly with respect to secondary boycotts.

The union's response to statutory limits on its traditional organizing techniques was to refine, rather than change, its approach in order to meet the letter of the law, and also to press recognition of previously negotiated "hot cargo" clauses. Prior to 1948, the Teamsters union had sought to include in its contracts clauses that enabled its members to refuse to cross picket lines and to refuse to handle "unfair goods" from firms engaged in a labor dispute. Such clauses acquired new significance when the National Labor Relations Board (NLRB) ruled that employers who agreed to such clauses were induced rather than coerced to "cease using, selling, handling, trans-

---

[17] Harry A. Millis and Emily Clark Brown, *From the Wagner Act to Taft-Hartley* (Chicago: University of Chicago Press, 1950), p. 247.

[18] James and James, *Hoffa and the Teamsters*, p. 14.

[19] U.S. Bureau of Labor Statistics, *Monthly Labor Review*, Vol. 4, No. 3 (March 1939), p. 508.

[20] U.S. Bureau of Labor Statistics, *Monthly Labor Review* Vol. 62, No. 4 (April 1946), p. 568.

porting or otherwise dealing" with another person and that such inducement was not unlawful under section 8(b)(4) of the Taft-Hartley Act.[21] The NLRB subsequently ruled in 1954 that such clauses were lawful only where employer compliance was voluntary rather than forced by the threat of concerted employee action.[22]

The nonenforceability of hot cargo clauses had relatively little practical effect on their value to the union in its organizing efforts. Jimmy Hoffa proved most adept at employing such clauses to secure ostensibly voluntary employer compliance in the 1950s. The key to his success was the desire of organized employers to maintain an amicable relationship, to avoid unnecessary problems under the union's open-ended grievance procedure, and to pressure their unorganized competitors. Thus, secondary boycott pressure continued to play a significant role in the union's organizing efforts and successes during the 1950s, particularly in the nonunion strongholds of Nebraska and the South.[23] Overall, these efforts and successes netted the union an additional 600,000 members by 1963, bringing its total reported membership to 1,500,000.[24]

THE DRIVE TO CENTRALIZE

The economic and institutional foundations from which the IBT developed were based upon local isolation and autonomy. In its first three decades, the union was little more than a loose confederation of local unions which had little economic incentive to coordinate their activities and which were characterized by a strong institutional aversion to centralized control. The local character of the trucking market made coordination unnecessary; the potential for local corruption, collusion, and personal gain made control unprofitable. Thus, it is hardly surprising that Daniel Tobin, the individual chosen to lead the international union from 1907 to 1952, was elected and reelected on an implicit platform of weak but honest leadership.[25]

The emergence of over-the-road trucking brought an end to the economic isolation of local unions but did not end their institutional independence. The result was a slow and grudging acceptance of the need both to extend the union's sights beyond the local delivery crafts and to coordinate local union activity on an area or regional

---

[21] James and James, *Hoffa and the Teamsters*, p. 144.
[22] *Ibid.*, p. 146.
[23] *Ibid.*, p. 147.
[24] *Ibid.*, p. 14.
[25] Garnel, *Rise of Teamster Power*, pp. 37-45.

basis in response to the changing character of the industry. The campaign for such adaptation originated not in the international union but in the efforts of two regional leaders, Dave Beck and Jimmy Hoffa, who led the long, hard struggle toward regional coordination. The battle was not won until Dave Beck succeeded Tobin as president of the international in 1952.

The real architect of the regional coordination was Jimmy Hoffa, who became an international union vice president in 1952 and succeeded Beck as president in 1957. During his tenure as vice president, Hoffa laid the foundation for the final step in the transformation of the union's traditional operating structure—the achievement of national coordination or, more accurately, control. In so doing he had to overcome strong institutional and economic forces that might easily have stymied a less determined and dominant leader, as indeed they have appeared to do to his successors since his departure from office in 1967. The system of national coordination and control that he built in the form of the National Master Freight Agreement (NMFA) remains in place to this day.

Regional Bargaining

The IBT's tradition of local autonomy and isolation constituted a formidable institutional barrier to the development of bargaining structures appropriate for over-the-road operations. The development of such structures was a long, slow process, beginning in the West in the early 1930s and culminating in the formation of the Eastern Conference in 1953. Despite growing regional organization, the union was still without a sound basis for national bargaining in the 1950s, a foundation that ultimately required another decade to build.

The challenge facing the union in the 1930s was to build multi-unit bargaining structures in the face of resistance from both employers and local unions. Beck and Dobbs directed their initial efforts toward coordinated bargaining in urban centers of power such as Seattle, and built outward to establish area and then statewide bargaining systems for over-the-road trucking. To minimize local union resistance, both men carefully avoided the inclusion of local cartage employees of over-the-road firms during this period.

The preexisting diversity in local wage rates and other terms and conditions constituted a serious potential problem in coordinated bargaining. That problem was solved by permitting such diversity to continue within the framework of common agreements. In the West, Beck focused his attention on common noneconomic terms to minimize employer resistance to Seattle wage levels.[26] In the Midwest, Dobbs and Hoffa pursued wage standardization more aggressively, but used what might be called a most favored nation approach to minimize local union resistance to the wage averaging demanded by standardization. The result in both cases was standard areawide and statewide agreements linked to a series of local riders that institutionalized special or superior local practices.

The evolution of regional bargaining structures followed much the same pattern of accommodation of diversity. The Western Conference, formed in 1937, remained localized well into the 1950s, isolated by distance from other conferences and characterized by strong local leaders in Seattle and San Francisco who jealously resisted centralization.[27] The Southern Conference, formed in 1943, did have a uniform agreement, but the agreement reflected the largely unorganized character of the region. The Midwestern Conference evolved from the Central States Drivers Council (CSDC) in 1953 when Ohio, long a member of the CSDC but not a signatory to its agreement, was brought into the fold by a deal that gave it the best of both the CSDC agreement and its own statewide agreement.[28] The Eastern Conference, also formed in 1953, was little more than a loose confederation that even five years later retained approximately twenty separate agreements.[29]

Before 1953, the Teamsters' various regional bargains and related supplemental agreements were almost totally independent of each other, and focused exclusively on over-the-road operations. The most notable exception was during the war years, when the War Labor Board used the Central States agreement as a pattern for the industry, particularly in the South.[30] In 1953, Jimmy Hoffa began to build on that precedent and to seek uniformity in wages between the Midwest and the South, where low wages exerted competitive pressure on the industry in the Central states. Within five years he was largely successful in achieving that goal, and also had succeeded in reducing the number of local riders in effect.[31] By 1955 he had forced the inclusion of local drivers employed by over-the-road firms in his regional agreements.[32]

---

[26] *Ibid.*, p. 84.
[27] Harold M. Levinson, *Determining Forces in Collective Wage Bargaining* (New York: John Wiley and Sons, 1966), pp. 229-30.
[28] James and James, *Hoffa and the Teamsters*, p. 119-22.
[29] Levinson, "Trucking," p. 115.
[30] Levinson, *Determining Forces in Collective Wage Bargaining*, pp. 228-29.
[31] *Ibid.*, p. 229.
[32] James and James, *Hoffa and the Teamsters*, pp. 126-27.

The wage standardization effort undertaken by Hoffa in the mid-1950s was not a simple task. Drivers in both the Central and Southern states were paid by miles (when driving) and hours (when not driving), but faced dissimilar operating conditions. Drivers in the Central states typically had to deal with shorter hauls, lower speeds, and more snow than drivers in the South, which meant that equal rates very often resulted in unequal earnings. Hoffa elected to equalize rates, which produced higher average hourly earnings for drivers in the South, perhaps as an inducement to unionize. Thus, the average hourly earnings of Class I line-haul drivers in the South increased from 88 percent of average hourly earnings in the Midwest in 1950, to 105 percent in 1958.[33] Over the same period, the intra-region dispersion of local cartage wage rates in both regions was dramatically reduced, as was the interregion differential in such rates, from 30 percent to 6 percent.[34]

Both the Western Conference and the highly fragmented Eastern Conference remained beyond Hoffa's control until 1961. Drivers in the West were paid on a miles or hours (whichever was greater) basis rather than a miles *and* hours basis, and typically were paid at lower mileage rates but higher hourly rates than drivers in the Central States, a practice reflecting easier driving conditions. The result was slightly higher average hourly earnings—10 percent in 1950 and 5 percent in 1958—for western line-haul drivers.[35] Drivers in the East were generally paid on an hourly or trip basis, and typically were paid at higher mileage rates, but lower hourly rates, than drivers in the Central states, which reflected more difficult driving conditions. This situation resulted in generally lower average hourly earnings—10 percent in 1950 and 1958—for eastern line-haul drivers.[36] In 1958, local cartage wages were lower in both the West and East, and were more widely dispersed than in the Central states or in the South.[37]

The centralization of bargaining structures begun by Beck and Dobbs in the 1930s, and carried on by Hoffa in the 1950s, had made substantial progress by the time Hoffa assumed the presidency of the union in 1957. Nevertheless, this centralization effort still fell far short of a national bargaining system; four regional bargaining structures remained in place, all four of which operated within the

---

[33] For a brief discussion of contingency of wage rates on driving conditions, see James and James, *Hoffa and the Teamsters*, pp. 321-35; for statistics, see Levinson, "Trucking," p. 117, Table 9.

[34] Levinson, "Trucking," p. 112, Table 5, and p. 113, Table 6.

[35] *Ibid.*, p. 117, Table 9.

[36] *Ibid.*

[37] *Ibid.*, pp. 112-13.

regional rate-making structure of the regulated industry. Of these regional structures, two were controlled by Hoffa and two were not. The former were characterized by a high degree of centralization in decision-making and standardization of terms and conditions; the latter two perpetuated local fragmentation and differentiation. Hoffa's goal, on assuming the union presidency, was to extend union control to the fragmented regions and to integrate them into a national bargaining system.

National Bargaining

Jimmy Hoffa held the presidency of the Teamsters until 1967, when he began to serve a thirteen-year prison sentence for jury-tampering and misuse of union pension funds. During his decade in office, he laid the foundation for a national system of bargaining as a supplement to, but not a substitute for, local and regional bargaining. That system, in the form of the National Master Freight Agreement, brought the industry and the union to the threshold of the "uniform wages, hours, and working conditions" envisioned by Dobbs when he formed the Central States Drivers Council in 1937, and Dobbs' goal might well have been reached had Hoffa continued to control the bargaining destiny of the union and the industry.

Hoffa assumed the presidency already in control of the regional bargaining systems in the Central states and the South. The West and East, however, were outside his control and thus constituted his major institutional challenge. The greatly fragmented East was inherently difficult to control, but not impossible to influence. The highly independent West was not as easily influenced, and ultimately had to be controlled by heavy-handed means. Such means were provided by a 1961 amendment of the union's constitution that empowered the international union president to appoint "international directors . . . to assist him in supervising and directing the activities" of area conferences, with which all local unions were required to affiliate, and to "assume the position of international director" himself, should he so desire, as Hoffa did in the case of the Western Area Conference in 1961.[38]

Hoffa used his influence in the East and his control in the West to make payment methods conform to the Central states' miles and hours system. In the East this meant phasing out the trip payment method; in the West, it meant replacing the miles or hours method. Hoffa also used his influence in the East to encourage consolidation of local agreements, and successfully produced a reduction in the

---

[38] IBT, *Proceedings, Eighteenth Convention*, p. 604.

number of such agreements from twenty-one in 1959 to twelve in 1972.[39] In conjunction with his efforts, Hoffa also achieved a reduction in the dispersion of both local cartage and over-the-road hourly mileage rates in the East, as he had done previously in the Midwest and South and would soon do in the West.[40]

The 1961 round of area trucking negotiations produced a set of agreements, patterned after the CSDC Agreement, that stipulated identical hourly rates for long-line drivers by 1963.[41] More significantly, most of these agreements contained language that paralleled CSDC over-the-road and local contracts, which stated:

> The parties in this Agreement accept the principle of a National Over-the-Road Agreement and are willing to enter into negotiations for the purpose of negotiating such National Agreement.[42]

Such language, and the constitutional changes made by the union at its 1961 convention, laid the groundwork for the first NMFA of 1964. The only missing element was a corresponding national organization of industry employers, a problem that was solved in 1963 by the formation of Trucking Employers Incorporated (TEI) to represent the industry in negotiations with the union. TEI represented the industry from 1964 to 1976, and claimed a membership that varied between 800 and 1,000 firms employing 300,000 to 500,000 unionized workers.[43]

The NMFA of 1964 was a major victory for Jimmy Hoffa in his drive to centralize bargaining. Procedurally the agreement constituted little more than a third tier in the existing system of regionally and locally negotiated agreements, but substantively it was far more significant, because it introduced both the principle and the practice of nationally negotiated changes in wage and benefit rates. As a result, control over both money and the trade-offs for which money is granted shifted to the national level. Much of the power of the IBT and TEI representatives in the NMFA negotiations was vested in this control, although each also held approval control over the regional supplements and riders to the NMFA.[44]

The NMFA of 1964 was a major milestone for the Teamsters in their efforts to organize the industry and to standardize wages. By 1964, the IBT had been largely successful in its ultimate goal of unionizing the industry and/or neutralizing nonunion competition,

---

[39] Levinson, "Trucking," p. 115, Table 7.
[40] *Ibid.*, pp. 112-13 and 115-16.
[41] James and James, *Hoffa and the Teamsters*, pp. 132-35 and 330-33.
[42] *Ibid.*, p. 135.
[43] Levinson, "Trucking," p. 105.
[44] *Ibid.*, pp. 106-08.

a goal obtained largely through the use of its secondary economic power. The IBT had also eliminated most of the basic structural differentials in compensation within the industry, and following ratification of the NMFA in 1964, continued to build an industry-wide bargaining structure through which remaining differentials could be narrowed, if not eliminated, through wage compression and benefit standardization.[45] In short, the IBT, largely as a result of the vision, persistence, and ingenuity of Jimmy Hoffa, all but succeeded in taking labor out of competition. The union could face the future with great confidence that given its primary and secondary economic power, it could keep both labor and labor costs (which together constitute 65 percent of total cost) out of competition in the trucking industry.

---

[45] *Ibid.*, pp. 111-18.

CHAPTER V

The Labor Relations of the Industry

In 1980 the trucking industry employed approximately 1.2 million people, a figure representing almost one-half the total number employed in transportation services at that time.[1] That number includes both local and intercity trucking workers, but does not include trucking employees of private carriers. No data on the number of such employees exist, but some insight into their number can be gained from the fact that of the more than 2,000,000 truck drivers employed in the United States in 1980, only 800,000 were employed in the trucking industry.[2]

Trucking is basically a blue-collar industry. Equal Employment Opportunity Commission (EEOC) data for trucking firms with 100 or more employees reveal that in 1981 more than 70 percent of trucking employees were classified as unskilled, semi-skilled, or skilled workers.[3] Given that fact, it is hardly surprising that the same data showed that women accounted for only 1.5 percent of all employees of such firms in 1981. EEOC data also reveal that trucking, at least in larger firms, is a predominantly white, male-dominated industry; in 1981, less than 15 percent of all employees in trucking firms with 100 or more employees were minorities, and about 75 percent of those were employed in unskilled or semi-skilled jobs.

BUREAU OF LABOR STATISTICS DATA

The trucking industry is generally regarded as a high-wage industry. In 1980 average hourly earnings in trucking were $9.33, as compared to $7.27 in all manufacturing, a differential of 28 percent (see Table V-1). The Bureau of Labor Statistics (BLS) has published

---

[1] Transportation Policy Associates, *Supplements, Updates, and Corrections to Transportation in America: A Statistical Analysis of Transportation in the United States* (Washington, D.C.: Transportation Policy Associates, November 1984), p. 19.

[2] U.S. Bureau of the Census, "Selected Characteristics of Employed Persons by Occupation, Industry and Sex, 1980," prepublication data in author's possession.

[3] U.S. Equal Employment Opportunity Commission data in author's possession.

TABLE V-1

Average Hourly Earnings
Trucking and All Manufacturing
1964–1980

Year	Trucking (dollars per hour)	Manufacturing (dollars per hour)	Trucking Wages as Percentage of Manufacturing Wages
1964	$3.02	$2.53	119
1965	3.13	2.61	120
1966	3.22	2.71	119
1967	3.29	2.82	117
1968	3.48	3.01	116
1969	3.69	3.19	116
1970	3.94	3.35	118
1971	4.52	3.57	127
1972	4.96	3.82	130
1973	5.39	4.09	132
1974	5.77	4.42	130
1975	6.12	4.83	127
1976	6.60	5.22	126
1977	7.23	5.68	127
1978	7.92	6.17	128
1979	8.51	6.70	127
1980	9.33	7.27	128

Source: U.S. Department of Labor, Bureau of Labor Statistics, *Employment, Hours, and Earnings, United States, 1909–84* (Washington, D.C.: Government Printing Office, March 1985), Vol. I, pp. 57–58 and Vol. II, p. 647.

data on average hourly earnings in trucking only since 1964. These data show a pattern of relatively modest increases (about 4 percent per year) in the late 1960s followed by far larger gains (9.25 percent per year) in the 1970s. As a result, wage gains in trucking paralleled those in manufacturing between 1965 and 1970, but substantially exceeded those in manufacturing between 1970 and 1980 (see Table V-1). The 1970-1973 period, in particular, saw a substantial rise in trucking wages relative to wages in all manufacturing.

Data available on average annual earnings and total compensation cost per full-time employee in the trucking industry prior to 1964 indicate that trucking was not a high-earnings industry vis-à-vis all manufacturing prior to the mid-1960s (see Table V-2). The data also suggest that trucking has not been a high-benefit industry vis-à-vis manufacturing, judging by the fact that positive differentials in compensation costs between trucking and manufacturing are consistently smaller (and negative differentials larger) than the coincident differentials in earnings.

TABLE V-2

Average Annual Earnings and Total Compensation Costs Trucking and Manufacturing 1950–1980

	Annual Earnings			Compensation Costs		
Year	Trucking	Manufacturing	Difference	Trucking	Manufacturing	Difference
1950	$ 3,469	$ 3,331	+$138	$ 3,629	$ 3,549	+$ 80
1955	4,409	4,482	− 73	4,690	4,855	− 165
1960	5,395	5,548	− 153	5,893	6,147	− 254
1965	6,625	6,566	+ 141	7,245	7,351	− 106
1970	8,672	8,381	+ 291	9,699	9,575	+ 124
1975	12,709	11,903	+ 806	14,673	14,180	+ 493
1980	18,864	17,966	+ 398	22,460	22,055	+ 405

Source: Transportation Policy Associates, *Transportation in America* (Washington, D.C.: Transportation Policy Associates, March 1983), p. 28.

COLLECTIVE BARGAINING

The balance of bargaining power in the trucking industry in the 1960s inherently favored the union. Individual employers, sheltered from the pressure of competition by growth, limited entry, collective ratemaking, and the organizing power of the Teamsters, had little compelling incentive to resist union demands. At the same time, they had little real ability to do so, given the industry's financial vulnerability to a strike. That situation was not fundamentally altered by multi-employer bargaining because

> [multi-employer bargaining] was not able to overcome the basic weakness inherent in the nature of the trucking industry. While it undoubtedly helped to provide greater continuity and perhaps unity among the larger firms, diversity of interests and slim financial resources continued to result in groups of carriers breaking away from the bargaining team and acceding to the union's demands.[4]

Wage Bargaining

The International Brotherhood of Teamsters (IBT) negotiated six National Master Freight Agreements (NMFAs) between 1964 and 1980. A chronology of the wage increases granted in these agreements indicates that three of the six agreements (1964, 1967, and

---

[4] Harold M. Levinson, "Trucking," in *Collective Bargaining: Contemporary American Experience*, ed. Gerald G. Somers (Madison Wis.: Industrial Relations Research Association, 1980), p. 106.

1973) produced moderate wage gains, while the other three (1970, 1976, and 1979) produced noticeably more substantial increases (see Table V-3). It also indicates that, with the exception of the 1964 agreement, percentage increases in hourly rates exceeded percentage increases in mileage rates. This pattern is consistent with the mix of local and over-the-road personnel that existed within the union's NMFA membership. It is also consistent with the fact that the earnings of local (hourly) personnel were far more dependent on base rates than were those of over-the-road (mileage) personnel, who can control such variables as speed and hours, and thereby mileage, to a degree that hourly personnel cannot.

The Teamsters union was led in its 1964 and 1967 NMFA negotiations by Jimmy Hoffa, who despite his problems with Federal authorities was firmly in control of the IBT during his tenure. That control enabled him to negotiate what were called two responsible settlements—settlements that achieved a balanced accommodation of the wishes of the industry and the desires of the union membership. These two settlements, particularly the 1967 settlement, were in retrospect too reasonable, since as a result average hourly earnings in trucking fell relative to those in manufacturing from 120 percent in 1965 to 116 percent in 1969. Thus, the IBT approached its 1970 NMFA negotiations with a catch-up problem not unlike

TABLE V-3

National Master Freight Agreement
Wage Chronology
1964–1982

	Hourly Rate			Mileage		
		Increase			Increase	
Agreement	Base (dollars per hour)	(dollars per hour)	(percent)	Base (dollars per hour)	(dollars per hour)	(percent)
1964	$3.03	$ .28	9.25	$10.03	$1.095	10.92
1967	3.31	.62	18.73	11.125	1.175	10.56
1970	3.93	2.01	51.15	12.300	3.150	25.61
1973	5.94	1.17	19.70	15.450	2.550	16.50
1976	7.11	2.27	31.90	18.000	5.050	28.06
1979	9.38	3.36	35.82	23.050	7.900	34.27

Source: *National Master Freight Agreement 1964–1982, Hourly & Mileage Rates & Increases and Fringe Benefits: Central States Supplements, Local Cartage Truck Driver & Tandem Axle 5-Axle Over-the-Road Driver* (March 15, 1982), prepared by Norman A. Weintraub, Chief Economist, International Brotherhood of Teamsters, Dept. of Economics.

those facing a number of unions whose 1967 settlements had failed to foresee the increasing inflation rates of the late 1960s.

The IBT entered NMFA negotiations in 1970 with a new leadership that had inherited the catch-up problem, but not the control of the union that Hoffa had held and might have been able to wield to achieve a tempered solution to that problem. The union leadership attempted to work out a solution, but the solution reached was unacceptable to the union's Local 705 in Chicago, which rejected the agreement and struck to force further negotiations. Local 705 ultimately succeeded in securing for its members additional increases in hourly wage rates, after which the union and the industry had no choice but to return to the bargaining table to negotiate a revised NMFA to match the additional gains won by the Chicago local. That NMFA wage agreement quickly halted and reversed the downward trend in the average hourly earnings differential between trucking and manufacturing. That differential, which stood at 16 percent in 1969, doubled to 32 percent by 1973.

The union entered its 1973 negotiations fairly well off. By then, its leadership was more firmly in control and more firmly committed to the wage/price control program. These conditions, coupled with a reduced rate of inflation, produced a responsible wage settlement that called for general wage increases averaging about 5 percent per year plus COLA capped at $0.22 over the term of the agreement. That settlement also proved too responsible in light of subsequent economic developments, and left the union leadership with a catch-up problem in 1976 similar to the one it had in 1970.

Both the 1976 and 1979 NMFA negotiations were conducted under the pressure of a union catch-up problem, and both resulted in fairly substantial wage settlements of approximately 30-35 percent. In 1976, the major problem was the cap on COLA under the 1973 contract; in 1979, the major problem was the COLA due but not paid for the final year of the 1976 contract. The latter problem was complicated by the existence of the Carter guidelines and by the fact that the IBT was in no mood to cooperate with the Carter administration, which by then had set a course toward trucking deregulation. Thus, the 1979 NMFA negotiations resulted in a three-way confrontation involving the union, the industry, and the government that culminated in a two-week strike before a trilaterally acceptable settlement was finally reached.

Wage increases and COLA payments (excluding the one due April 1, 1982) under the 1976 and 1979 NMFAs brought the basic hourly wage rate of Teamster NMFA members to $12.74 by mid-1981. That rate was more than 25 percent higher than average hourly earnings in all trucking, and almost 50 percent higher than average hourly earnings in all manufacturing; in 1964, those two differentials were 4 and 24 percent, respectively. Thus, the IBT was obviously successful, between 1964 and 1981, in putting some distance between its NMFA members and the rest of the trucking industry in terms of hourly wage rates.

Benefit Bargaining

Benefit bargaining under the NMFA traditionally has been focused on two basic benefit plans—pensions and health and welfare. Both are defined as contribution rather than benefit plans, so bargaining usually focuses on employer contributions to the benefit funds. Increases in employer contributions to these funds have been significant; prior to the 1964 agreement, unionized employers in the Central states contributed a total of $9.50 per week ($0.2375 per hour) to these funds, but by 1981, that total had grown almost tenfold, to $90.50 per week ($2.2625 per hour). Growth in NMFA employer benefit costs in the first six NMFAs is traced in Table V-4.

The data on employer benefit contributions reveal a significantly greater rate of increase in benefit costs (735 percent) than in wage rates (400 percent) between 1964 and 1982. This pattern characterized the terms of all but the 1970 NMFA, but the difference was most pronounced during the 1973 agreement, when benefit costs increased by 70 percent. The following two agreements did not match that rate of increase, but did, in combination, result in a doubling of benefit costs, with most of that increase attributable to increases in pension contributions.

Overall, total NMFA compensation costs (wages plus benefit contributions) more than quadrupled between 1963 and 1982 (see Table V-5). That growth was the product of average annual increases of about 5 percent during the 1964-1969 period and of about 10 percent during the 1970-1975 and 1976-1981 periods. The relatively more rapid rise in benefit costs than wage costs in each of these periods produced a gradual increase in benefit costs as a percentage of total compensation cost from 7.3 percent in 1963 to 11.0 percent in 1969, and from 13.3 percent in 1975 to 15.1 percent in 1981.

The doubling of benefit costs as a percentage of compensation costs between 1963 and 1981 did not make NMFA carriers high benefit cost employers vis-à-vis industries such as auto or steel. It may, however, have made them high benefit cost producers within the trucking industry. The only data on benefit costs of non-NMFA carriers appears in a 1973 Council on Wage and Price Stability

TABLE V-4

NMFA Benefit Contributions
1964–1982

Agreement	Pension			Welfare			Total		
	Base (dollars per hour)	Increase (dollars per hour)	(percent)	Base (dollars per hour)	Increase (dollars per hour)	(percent)	Base (dollars per hour)	Increase (dollars per hour)	(percent)
1964	$ 6.00	$ 2.00	33.3	$ 3.50	$ 3.80	108.6	$ 9.50	$ 5.80	61.1
1967	8.00	2.00	25.0	7.30	2.20	30.1	15.30	4.20	27.5
1970	10.00	3.00	30.0	9.50	3.00	31.6	19.50	6.00	30.8
1973	13.00	9.00	69.2	12.50	9.00	72.0	25.50	18.00	70.6
1976	22.00	9.00	40.9	21.50	8.00	37.2	43.50	17.00	39.1
1979	31.00	20.00	64.5	29.50	10.00	33.9	60.50	30.00	49.6
1982	51.00	—	—	39.50	—	—	90.50	—	—

Source: *National Master Freight Agreement 1964–1982, Hourly & Mileage Rates & Increases and Fringe Benefits: Central States Supplements, Local Cartage Truck Driver & Tandem Axle 5-Axle Over-the-Road Driver* (March 15, 1982), prepared by Normal A. Weintraub, Chief Economist, International Brotherhood of Teamsters, Dept. of Economics.

TABLE V-5

NMFA Hourly Wages and Benefits
1964–1981

Year	Wages	Benefits	Total	Percent Increase	
				Annual	Contract
1963	$ 3.03	$ .2375	$3.2675		
1964	3.13	.3075	3.4375	5.2	13.5
1965	3.21	.3450	3.5555	3.4	
1966	3.31	.3825	3.6930	3.7	
1967	3.56	.4375	3.9980	8.3	19.6
1968	3.74	.4625	4.2030	5.1	
1969	3.93	.4875	4.4180	5.1	
1970	4.43	.5375	4.8680	12.5	44.4
1971	5.16	.5875	5.4780	15.7	
1972	5.74	.3675	6.3780	10.9	
1973	6.29	.8375	7.1280	11.8	28.5
1974	6.70	.9625	7.6630	7.5	
1975	7.11	1.0875	8.1980	7.0	
1976	7.76	1.2375	8.9980	9.6	34.2
1977	8.50	1.3375	9.9860	11.0	
1978	9.38	1.5125	11.0010	10.2	
1979	10.67	1.8625	12.9670	15.4	36.4
1980	11.97	2.0625	14.2630	12.3	
1981	12.74	2.2625	15.0025	5.2	

Source: *National Master Freight Agreement 1964–1982, Hourly & Mileage Rates &*
Increases and Fringe Benefits: Central States Supplements, Local Cartage
Truck Driver & Tandem Axle 5-Axle Over-the-Road Driver (March 15, 1982),
prepared by Norman A. Weintraub, Chief Economist, International Brotherhood of Teamsters, Dept. of Economics.

report indicating that benefit costs in the unionized sector of the
trucking industry represented about 15 percent of total labor cost,
as compared to 10 percent for the industry as a whole.[5] The fact
that this differential is built upon a differential in hourly earnings
suggests the possibility of a significant absolute hourly benefit cost
differential within the trucking industry.

Productivity Bargaining

The NMFA is largely devoid of detailed provisions regarding
workrules. Those rules historically have been, and for the most part
remain, embodied in regional or local agreements. There is consid-

---

[5] Council on Wage and Price Stability, *1976 Collective Bargaining Negotiations*
(Washington, D.C.: Executive Office of the President, January 1976), p. 61.

erable diversity in the provisions of the various regional supplements to the NMFA with respect to workrules, but some consistency exists in four areas. First, regional supplements generally contain maintenance of standards clauses that institutionalize prevailing area and local practices. Second, regional supplements traditionally contain terminal-to-terminal rules that institutionalize the division of labor between local and over-the-road drivers in general freight carriage by banning direct pickup and/or delivery by over-the-road drivers. Third, the supplements contain special commodity riders that permit general freight carriers to operate separate special commodity operations that are not subject to the terminal-to-terminal rule. Finally, supplements typically contain provisions regarding pay guarantees and minimums for drivers that shift the burden of less-than-optimal scheduling of runs from drivers to carriers.

The fact that most workrules are set regionally or locally does not mean that such issues are beyond national attention or negotiation. Regional and local supplements to the NMFA are technically subject to national union and management approval, and unresolved issues in negotiations over such supplements are subject to resolution in NMFA negotiations. In theory, the linkage between national negotiation of wages and benefits and sub-national negotiation of workrules should create the possibility of trade-offs and/or buy-outs in national bargaining. In practice, however, such trade-offs have been rare because the system leaves deadlocked issues to be resolved at the highest negotiating levels after, not before, economic issues have been settled, when "the parties are tired, and the employers have little stomach to face a strike on issues which often affect only a few localities."[6] Thus, the system has worked to give added meaning and strength to the maintenance of standards clause as a potential barrier to change in the status quo with respect to operations.

The NMFA is not entirely silent on the subject of changing operations. It contains its own maintenance of standards clause, which tacitly recognizes and accepts the possibility of regional and local special arrangements possibly resulting in substandard working conditions. More important, the NMFA contains a provision that deals directly with "change of operations," and requires that "present terminals, breaking points, or domiciles shall not be transferred or changed without the approval of an appropriate change of operations committee ... equally composed of employer and union

---

[6] Levinson, "Trucking," p. 141.

representatives."[7] In theory, this provision gives the union the power to prevent any major change in the operating structure of signatory carriers. In practice, the union has exercised that power in a manner some have called "consistently moderate and adaptive."[8] Such adaptive behavior may be explained in part by another NMFA provision that requires that "when a new terminal(s) is opened ... the employer shall offer to those employees, if any, affected ... the opportunity to transfer to regular positions in the new terminal(s)."[9]

The NMFA contains one other better-known contractual restriction—the trailer-on-flatcar rule. Under this rule, signatory carriers are not prevented from substituting rail for road movement of freight over their established routes, but are required to compensate any driver available to move the freight in question at point of origin or any relay point for the work he would have done.[10] The result of this provision has been to severely constrain, but not eliminate, piggybacking by NMFA carriers, which has placed them at a potential competitive disadvantage vis-à-vis other carriers not so constrained.

---

[7] National Master Freight Agreement for April 1, 1979 through March 31, 1982, article 8, section 6.

[8] Levinson, "Trucking," p. 141.

[9] National Master Freight Agreement for April 1, 1979 through March 31, 1982, article 8, section 6(d)(3).

[10] *Ibid.*

CHAPTER VI

The Deorganization of the Industry

The National Master Freight Agreement (NMFA) of 1964 was a milestone in the Teamsters' drive to take trucking labor out of competition. It also may have marked the high point in that drive. After 1964, growing legal and logistical constraints on the union's organizing power slowly but surely loosened its control over the industry. The result was the growth of nonunion trucking operations, which by 1979 had reached the point at which "the most crucial collective bargaining problem facing the parties [was] a clear downward trend in the share of freight being moved over the highway by Teamster members."[1] Estimates of the magnitude of that trend suggested "that the volume of freight being handled by the union had declined by approximately 20-25 percent over the decade 1967-77."[2]

TEAMSTER ORGANIZING POWER

Historically, the key to the power of the Teamsters in gaining recognition and/or securing adherence to union standards was its ability to both threaten and apply secondary economic pressure on recalcitrant employers. The effectiveness of this weapon was not much impaired by the provisions of the Taft-Hartley Act of 1947, which was designed to limit secondary boycott activity. This was not the case, however, under the expanded proscriptions against such activity embodied in the Landrum-Griffin Act of 1959.

The legal restraints on secondary boycott activity were important in their own right, but took on added significance because of structural changes in trucking activity that produced substantial increases in employment in those areas in which the union faced its greatest institutional problems in organizing by ballot rather than boycott. These structural changes included the more rapid growth of special commodity traffic relative to general freight traffic and

---

[1] Harold M. Levinson, "Trucking," in *Collective Bargaining: Contemporary American Experience*, ed. Gerald G. Somers (Madison, Wis.: Industrial Relations Research Association, 1980), p. 135.

[2] *Ibid.*

greater expansion in private carriage relative to for-hire carriage. These two trends reportedly produced a decline of 40 percent in the ratio of general freight carrier trucks to total trucks on the road between 1965 and 1980.[3] Accompanying these changes was a dramatic expansion in the role of owner-operators; between 1972 and 1980, self-employment in the industry grew by an estimated 43 percent compared to an increase of 15 percent in overall industry employment.[4]

Statutory Constraints

Crucial to successful Teamster pursuit of a top-down organizing strategy was its ability to impede the pickup or delivery of freight by nonunion trucking personnel. To do so, the union had to convince either employees or employers to refuse to handle freight tendered or claimed by such personnel. The two strategic devices at its disposal to achieve this end were ambulatory picketing and hot cargo clauses. Both of these devices were used effectively by the union in the 1950s to resist the rise and restrict the range of nonunion carriers. Their role in the organizational successes of the union in those years has been characterized as follows:

> The use of secondary pressure and "hot cargo" clauses [were] an important method by which Hoffa had not only protected the jurisdiction of the union but also extended it to employers far removed from his primary locus of power; even more important, they provided an impenetrable defense against encroachment of nonunion carriers in strongly held union areas.[5]

Such activities violated the spirit of section 8(b)(4)(A) of the Taft-Hartley Act, but not the letter of that section of the law as interpreted by the National Labor Relations Board (NLRB) and the courts. In 1959, Congress amended the letter of the law on secondary boycotts to better effectuate the intent of the original section 8(b)(4)(A). Specifically, Congress declared it to be an unfair labor practice for a union to induce or encourage individual employees, or to coerce or restrain persons engaged in commerce, to cease handling or transporting the products of any other producer [section 8(b)(4)(A)], and made it unlawful for unions and employers to enter

---

[3] U.S. General Accounting Office, "Effects of Regulatory Reform on Unemployment in the Trucking Industry," Report to the Honorable Dennis DeConcini, U.S. Senate (Gaithersburg, Md.: Government Printing Office, CED-82-90, June 11, 1982), Appendix I, p. 13.

[4] *Ibid.*

[5] Levinson, "Trucking," p. 136.

into contracts under which the employer agrees to cease or refrain from handling the products of any other employer [section 8(e)].

These changes in the law severely curtailed the union's ability to utilize its organizational base to impede the activities of nonunion firms. Union employees and employers could no longer refuse to load or unload freight carried by nonunion drivers without risk of legal penalties, and secondary picketing of nonunion trucks and drivers also was subject to tighter control with respect to both its conduct and consequences. When the full force of these changes was felt in the mid-1960s, the Teamsters union had to become more cautious in exerting secondary pressure on nonunion firms. This enabled such firms to expand their operations into new areas "by acquiring new operating rights, assigning nonunion drivers (often owner-operators) to newly established runs, and opening new terminals with nonunion personnel."[6]

The advent of administrative deregulation in 1977 should have served to facilitate such expansion by nonunion carriers, and indeed, that does appear to have been the case. The General Accounting Office (GAO) reported that between 1978 and 1980 the percentage of union drivers for regular route common carriers dropped from 84.3 to 75.3 percent, while the percentage of owner-operator drivers for general freight carriers increased from 2 to 14 percent.[7] A question on predominant union representation status in the Wharton Industrial Research Unit questionnaire of common carriers produced an even more dramatic picture of the possible extent of the erosion of unionization by the early 1980s (see Table VI-1).

Structural Change

The heart of the Teamsters' organizational strength in trucking historically has been among regular route carriers of general freight operating in the less-than-truckload market. Since 1965, and particularly since 1970, most of the growth in trucking has occurred among irregular route carriers, contract carriers, and special commodity divisions of general freight carriers, all of which are predominantly truckload carriers that rely heavily on owner-operators. This pattern of growth was reflected in the fact that Teamster general freight carrier employment remained relatively constant between 1972 and 1980, while industry employment grew by 15 percent and industry self-employment by 43 percent.[8]

---

[6] *Ibid.*
[7] U.S. General Accounting Office, "Effects of Regulatory Reform," p. 13.
[8] *Ibid.*

TABLE VI-1

Predominant Union Representation by
Percent of Responding Firms, 1983

	Drivers and Helpers (percent)	Vehicle Maintenance (percent)	Cargo Handlers (percent)
Nonunion	44	42	69
Union	56	58	31
Teamsters	49	43.5	25
Machinists	1	10	0
Other AFL-CIO	4	3	5
Independent	2	1.5	1
Teamsters as Percent of Total Union	87.5	75	80

Source: Industrial Research Unit questionnaire, 1983.

Owner-Operators. The chief organizing problem confronting the IBT in the growing truckload segment of the industry in the 1970s was the extensive reliance of truckload carriers on owner-operators, who historically have resisted unionization. This problem persisted for the Teamsters through the end of the 1970s, at which time the union admitted that it represented "only about 20,000, or 10 percent of, owner-operators."[9] The union acknowledged that its lack of organizing success among owner-operators was partly a function of the owner-operators' independent, entrepreneurial character, and pointed to the fact that in certain situations the law considers owner-operators independent contractors rather than employees. As such, owner-operators often are denied the protection of the National Labor Relations Act with respect to the right to organize and to bargain collectively, which, according to the Teamsters, forces the union into a "very difficult and costly legal battle in attempting to organize owner-operators where the company has structured the operation to avoid unionization."[10] Regardless of the reason, the union's lack of success in organizing owner-operators has resulted in a population of drivers for irregular route common carriers and contract carriers that in 1980 was only 19 percent unionized, down from 27 percent in 1978.[11]

Private Carriage. The "shadow sector" of the industry and the truckload market—private carriage—also grew substantially during the late 1960s and 1970s, and Teamster efforts to organize private carrier trucking employees, like those to organize owner-

---

[9] *Ibid.,* pp. 14-15.
[10] *Ibid.,* p. 15.
[11] *Ibid.,* p. 13.

TABLE VI-2

Predominant Union Representation
in Private and Common Carriers
by Percent of Responding Firms, 1983

	Drivers and Helpers		Vehicle Maintenance		Cargo Handlers	
	private carriers	common carriers	private carriers	common carriers	private carriers	common carriers
	(percent)		(percent)		(percent)	
Nonunion	42	44	69	42	55	69
Union	58	56	31	58	45	31
Teamsters	34	49	14	44	16	25
Machinists	0	1	3	10	0	0
Other AFL-CIO	12	4	13	1	28	5
Independent	12	2	1	1	0	1
Teamsters as Percent of Total Union	58.6	87.5	45.2	75.9	35.6	80.6

Source: Industrial Research Unit questionnaire, 1983.

operators, encountered some special institutional and legal problems. Institutionally, the IBT often had to compete with unions that represented or sought to represent production employees in a firm in its efforts to win bargaining rights for that firm's trucking workers. Legally, the IBT was often thwarted in its efforts to organize private carrier trucking employees by the fact that "the National Labor Relations Board will not certify a private company's trucking operations as an appropriate labor bargaining unit if the drivers also perform other company functions," thereby enabling companies "to avoid Teamsters' efforts to organize their trucking employees by giving their drivers other company tasks to perform."[12]

Few data exist on the unionization of private carrier trucking employees, but data reported by the GAO do indicate that 25 to 30 percent of private carrier drivers were organized in the late 1970s.[13] The results of the Industrial Research Unit questionnaire of private carriers suggest a similar figure, approximately 33 percent, but also indicate that the Teamsters union was not the same dominant force in the unionized segment of private carriage that it was in common carriage (see Table VI-2). In that context, it may also be noted that only one-quarter of the unionized private carriers responding to the questionnaire indicated that any of their trucking operations were subject to the NMFA.

[12] *Ibid.*, p. 14.
[13] *Ibid.*, p. 13.

TEAMSTER BARGAINING POWER

The gradual erosion of Teamster organizing power and control between 1967 and 1977 did not affect their bargaining power vis-à-vis unionized carriers. The extent to which the union chose or was compelled to utilize its bargaining power in NMFA negotiations over that period was discussed earlier in this study, as was the pattern of settlements resulting from these negotiations. The most significant aspect of these settlements relates not to their pattern but to their cumulative effect in creating a substantial wage differential between NMFA carriers and the industry average, which by 1980 approached 20 percent (see Table VI-3).

The growing wage gap between NMFA carriers and the trucking industry is likely a product of two factors: a growing absolute wage

TABLE VI-3

Average Hourly Wage Rates
NMFA and Trucking
1964–1980

Teamsters		Trucking		Teamster Wage Rate as Percentage of Trucking Wage Rate
Year*	Wage	Year*	Wage	
1964	3.13	1965	3.13	100.0
1965	3.21	1966	3.22	99.7
1966	3.31	1967	3.29	100.6
1967	3.56	1968	3.48	102.3
1968	3.74	1969	3.69	101.4
1969	3.93	1970	3.94	99.7
1970	4.43	1971	4.52	98.0
1971	5.16	1972	4.96	104.0
1972	5.74	1973	5.39	106.5
1973	6.29	1974	5.77	109.0
1974	6.70	1975	6.12	109.5
1975	7.11	1976	6.60	107.7
1976	7.76	1977	7.23	107.3
1977	8.50	1978	7.92	107.3
1978	9.38	1979	8.51	110.2
1979	10.67	1980	9.33	114.4
1980	11.97	1981	10.11	118.4

Source: U.S. Department of Labor, Bureau of Labor Statistics, *Employment, Hours, and Earnings, United States, 1909–84* (Washington, D.C.: Government Printing Office, March 1985), Volume II, p. 647; and *National Master Freight Agreement 1964–1982, Hourly & Mileage Rates & Increases and Fringe Benefits: Central States Supplements, Local Cartage Truck Driver & Tandem Axle 5-Axle Over-the-Road Driver* (March 15, 1982), prepared by Normal A. Weintraub, Chief Economist, International Brotherhood of Teamsters, Dept. of Economics.

* Trucking rates lagged one year because of effective dates of Teamster contracts.

TABLE VI-4

Open Shop Relative Wages, 1983

Percent of Employees Paid Union Rates	Percent of Open Shop Responding Firms
0–9	9.3
10–19	8.2
20–29	7.2
30–39	6.2
40–49	1.0
Less than 50	31.9
50–59	7.2
60–69	6.2
70–79	11.3
80–89	6.2
00 00	5.2
100	32.0
More than 50	68.1

Source: Industrial Research Unit questionnaire, 1983.

differential between NMFA and non-NMFA wage rates; and a growing ratio of non-NMFA to NMFA employees in the industry. There is no way to discern the relative importance of these two factors, because no data exist on the distribution of wage rates for non-NMFA trucking industry personnel, although the Industrial Research Unit questionnaire of common carriers did generate some rudimentary data on that distribution (see Table VI-4). No data exist on the total number of workers employed under the terms and conditions of the NMFA, but the number of workers directly covered by that agreement reportedly dropped from 306,037 under the 1970 contract to 277,017 under the 1979 contract, a drop of about 9.5 percent, compared to a growth rate in total industry employment over the period of about 20 percent.[14]

The Roots of Nonunion Competition

The results of the Industrial Research Unit questionnaire confirmed the existence of widespread open shop competition at the end of the 1970s. Fully 97 percent of the respondents to the questionnaire indicated that they competed directly with open shop carriers. Approximately 50 percent of those respondents indicated that they were not faring well in that competition by reporting substantial (20 to 50 percent) losses of business to their open shop competitors.

---

[14] *Ibid.*, p. 12.

The responding carriers were divided on the question of when their competition with open shop carriers began. Fully 60 percent indicated that their competition with nonunion carriers began prior to the advent of administrative deregulation in 1977. Another 25 percent related the origins of such competition to administrative deregulation. Only 15 percent attributed the roots of open shop competition to the passage of the MCA.

A number of firms indicated multiple dates of origin of open shop competition in patterns that suggest an intensification of such competition concurrent with the advent and advance of deregulation. This interpretation is supported by the fact that 70 percent of the respondents strongly agreed that there had been an increase in open shop competition after deregulation. A similar percentage of respondents indicated that the increase in open shop competition was primarily attributable to deregulation, but almost one-half of the respondents indicated that an increase in open shop competition would have taken place without deregulation (but not necessarily at the same rate).

When this study was being prepared it was hoped that carrier operating data and records of contribution to health and welfare and pension funds, which Class I and Class II common carriers are required to report to the ICC, could be used to provide a clearer picture of the pattern of growth of open shop trucking from 1974 to 1977 (prior to administrative deregulation) and from 1977 to 1980 (under administrative deregulation). By the time this study was begun, however, the data were no longer accessible within the ICC, which consequently was unable to make them available. The ICC could provide only the 1979 carrier operating data as a basis for assessing the growth of open shop trucking prior to passage of the MCA, and this fact precludes any attempt to discern the effect of administrative deregulation on the deorganization of the industry.

The ICC operating data for 1979 indicate that the deorganization of the industry had proceeded very far prior to passage of the MCA with respect to the large Class I carriers, but had been most substantial among the smaller Class II carriers. Of 332 Class I carriers reporting data on benefit fund contributions, only 16 (less than 5 percent) reported no such contributions, making them "nonunion carriers." The remaining 316 union carriers contributed an average of about $2,650 per employee to such funds, about 75 percent of the amount required by the 1976 and 1979 NMFAs. That percentage approximates the percentage of large carrier employment comprised by production workers, which suggests that the large carriers remained, for the most part, completely unionized. The data for

Class II carriers, however, present quite the opposite picture. Of 1,895 carriers reporting data on benefit fund contributions, only 323 (less than 20 percent) reported making any such contributions. Thus, almost 83 percent of all Class II carriers in 1979 appear to have been open shop carriers.[15]

Results of Nonunion Competition

By 1977, the ranks of nonunion carriers had grown to the point where they constituted a serious competitive threat to the survival of many smaller unionized carriers. The carriers facing the greatest competitive pressure were those operating in short-haul markets, whose labor costs are determined by hourly wage rates to a far greater extent than is the case for long-haul carriers, for whom mileage rates are key. The economic interests of short-haul carriers were not well served by the relatively greater increases in hourly rates than in mileage rates that were negotiated by Trucking Employers Incorporated (TEI) beginning with the 1970 NMFA. The 1976 NMFA did little to alleviate the special problems of short-haul carriers, which led many to withdraw from TEI and eventually caused the breakup of that multiemployer bargaining organization in 1077.

The withdrawal of the smaller short-haul carriers from TEI was dictated by the smaller carriers' desire to free themselves in collective bargaining from the domination of the larger long-haul carriers, who did not need to address the problem of nonunion competition that smaller carriers were being forced to confront. The smaller carriers that withdrew from TEI hoped to create a two-tier bargaining system involving separate, independent negotiations for short-haul carriers that would produce lower hourly wage increases and less restrictive work rules. Such a bargaining system was not acceptable to the union, however, which left the short-haul carriers no real choice but to live with a one-tier system of NMFA negotiations in 1979. These negotiations were conducted for the industry by Trucking Management Incorporated (TMI) on behalf of most, but not all, of the carriers previously represented by TEI.

The failure of the smaller carriers to find a forum for consideration of their special competitive problems at the national level precluded efforts to create a forum at the regional or local level. The carriers in question wanted to develop a set of regional "short-haul riders" comparable to the special-commodity riders in the NMFA system, but the union was not receptive to that approach,

---

[15] ICC databank of trucking industry statistics.

and as a result the carriers were forced to seek special consideration at the local level. The union typically has frowned upon local concessions to requests for special consideration at both the national and regional levels, but this apparently did not deter local unions from taking such action with or without formal union sanction. Thus, by the late 1970s the growing nonunion threat to smaller carriers reportedly had led to

> the spread of various "under the table" arrangements made by local unions with many individual companies or groups of smaller companies under which the officially negotiated wage-fringe standards are being quietly undercut.[16]

Such special consideration is not without ample precedent in the history of the highly pragmatic Teamsters union and has generally not constituted a serious threat to the integrity of union standards because such consideration has been granted only as a last-ditch measure to save a carrier in dire financial distress. At the end of the 1970s, however, the situation was somewhat different, in that instances of special consideration became common practice in some areas, which suggested the possibility of "a growing recognition within the union that more broadly based policies of adjustment" might be in order.[17] No such policies were evident in the outcome of the 1979 NMFA negotiations, which indicated that the erosion of the union's organizational control of the industry had not yet reached the point in the eyes of its membership (if not its leadership) to justify constraint on the exercise of the union's still formidable bargaining power over the sizeable, if shrinking, unionized segment of the industry.

---

[16] Levinson, "Trucking," p. 139.
[17] *Ibid.*

CHAPTER VII

The Deregulation of the Industry

The deregulation of intercity for-hire trucking formally occurred on July 1, 1980, when President Carter signed into law the Motor Carrier Act (MCA) of 1980. The origins of the MCA can be traced back almost two decades, to the Kennedy administration, but the seed of deregulation planted at that time lay dormant until the mid-1970s, when it was nurtured and brought to flower by the Carter administration.

The seed of deregulation was a congressional study of motor carrier regulation published in 1961, a time when the trucking industry and the International Brotherhood of Teamsters (IBT or Teamsters) were subject to widespread public and political disfavor. The 1961 study was highly critical of the existing system of regulation, and called for

> a reorientation of regulatory thinking in respect to motor common carrier authorizations [that] is long overdue.... We recognize that rationalization of the presently fragmented and confused situation will be a long, expensive, and often painful undertaking. We believe it necessary in our national interest and that it will repay a hundredfold the effort and investment required.[1]

The call for regulatory reform was soon drowned out by subsequent events, however, and was not answered in the 1960s—a decade in which regulation, not deregulation, was the chosen course.

The early 1970s brought the return of a Republican to the White House and produced considerable discussion, but little action, regarding deregulation in general, and deregulation in trucking in particular. White House policy favored deregulation of trucking and confrontation with the IBT in 1962, but in 1972, the White House chose to pursue the opposite course. Five years later, however, the Carter administration set out on the road toward trucking deregulation.

In response to the 1973-1974 energy crisis, precedent and mo-

---

[1] U.S. Senate Committee on Commerce, Special Study Group on Transportation Policies of the United States, *National Transportation Policy Report*, S. Rep. No. 445, 87th Congress, 1st Sess. (1961) (Washington, D.C.: U.S. Government Printing Office, 1961), p. 550.

mentum for administrative deregulation were established by an easing of Interstate Commerce Commission (ICC) route restrictions on common carriers. This enabled irregular route carriers to ignore gateway restrictions and regular route carriers to deviate from their prescribed routes as long as the resulting reduction in mileage did not exceed 20 percent of normal route mileage.[2] The regulatory route pursued by the Carter administration remained administrative rather than legislative, but the policy changes undertaken by the Carter administration were far more profound and qualitatively different than those effected in 1973 and 1974. The General Accounting Office (GAO) characterized the changes made during the Carter years in the following terms:

> The Interstate Commerce Commission (ICC) took administrative steps to reduce the regulatory framework in the trucking industry well before the Motor Carrier Act. Beginning in 1977, ICC under its own authority eased entry policy, relaxed certain restrictions on carriers' existing route systems and operations, and expanded the area carriers can serve.[3]

The first significant change in ICC policy came in April 1977, when the ICC drastically expanded the commercial zones within which trucking operations were exempt from federal control.[4] The commission subsequently repealed its "rule of eight" and began to allow contract carriers to serve more than eight shippers.[5] The most important policy changes during Carter's term, however, were in the area of entry.[6] The commission streamlined the process of applying for operating authority and narrowed the ability of existing firms to challenge applications for new authority by shifting the burden of proof of serving the public interest from the applicant to the protestor. In addition, the commission changed its policy and permitted for-hire firms to hold both common and contract authority, and also allowed private carriers to act as common carriers in certain limited circumstances.

These changes in ICC entry rules and procedures produced a clear upward trend in the number of operating authority applications, from 6,800 in fiscal year 1976 to 12,800 in fiscal year 1979. They

---

[2] Interstate Commerce Commission, *88th Annual Report to Congress, 1974* (Washington, D.C.: U.S. Government Printing Office, June 11, 1982), pp. 5-6.

[3] U.S. General Accounting Office, *Effects of Regulatory Reform on Unemployment in the Trucking Industry* (Washington, D.C.: U.S. General Accounting Office, June 11, 1982), p. 1.

[4] Interstate Commerce Commission, *91st Annual Report to Congress, 1977* (Washington, D.C.: U.S. Government Printing Office, 1977), p. 54.

[5] Interstate Commerce Commission, *92nd Annual Report to Congress, 1978* (Washington, D.C.: U.S. Government Printing Office, 1978), p. 1.

[6] *Ibid.*, pp. 49-51.

also produced a parallel upward trend in the percentage of such applications approved in whole or part, from 70 percent in 1976 to 95 percent in 1979. Despite such trends, however, a 1979 study by the Department of Transportation concluded that the impact of revised entry policies on competition had been negligible for three reasons. First, most of the applications and awards were for extensions of authority; applications by, and grants to, new carriers did not increase significantly. Second, the procedural and policy changes on challenges to applications weakened but did not eliminate the threat of such challenges, with their attendant delays and legal costs, as a deterrent to entry. Third, new grants of authority remained narrow and were restricted to specific shippers and/or commodities.[7]

The trucking industry had quite a different viewpoint on the real or potential competitive effects of the ICC's "steps to reduce the regulatory framework in the trucking industry." The industry, in the form of the American Trucking Associations (ATA), denounced these steps in public and challenged them in the courts, but with little or no success. After numerous defeats in the courts, the carriers asked Senator Howard Cannon, chairman of the Senate Committee on Science and Transportation, to intercede with the ICC on their behalf on the grounds that the commission was usurping power that only Congress possessed to deregulate transportation. At Cannon's request, the commission suspended its regulatory reforms pending an act of Congress. Congress responded with the passage of the MCA of 1980.

In retrospect, the framing of the act makes clear that established industry members found few friends in Congress. It is equally clear that the industry subsequently had few friends in the ICC when the commission interpreted and implemented the act. As a result, the industry once again was forced to return to the courts. By June 1982, "approximately 170 court cases involving motor carrier licensing" had been filed.[8]

THE MOTOR CARRIER ACT OF 1980

Section 4 of the MCA of 1980 declares that the act embodies national transportation policy "with respect to transportation of

---

[7] U.S. Department of Transportation, Office of Transportation Policy, "New Entry in the Regulated Motor Carrier Industry," December 19, 1979, Contract No. DOT-OS-80047, Task Order 4, pp. 4-5.

[8] Reese H. Taylor, Jr., Statement on the Implementation of the Motor Carrier Act of 1980 before the Subcommittee on Surface Transportation of the House Committee on Public Works and Transportation, June 23, 1982, Appendix II, p. 1. (transcript in author's possession).

property by motor carrier to promote competitive and efficient transportation services."[9] The purpose of this policy is to

> (A) meet the needs of shippers, receivers, and consumers; (B) allow a variety of quality and price options to meet changing market demands and the diverse requirements of the shipping public; (C) allow the most productive use of equipment and energy resources; (D) enable efficient and well-managed carriers to earn adequate profits, attract capital, and maintain fair wages and working conditions.[10]

Section 3 of the act acknowledges that the system of motor carrier regulation existing before the MCA was "outdated" and had to be "revised to reflect the transportation needs and realities of the 1980's."[11] Specifically, Congress found the system deficient in promoting competitive and efficient transportation services:

> Historically the existing regulatory structure has tended in certain circumstances to inhibit market entry, carrier growth, maximum utilization of equipment and energy resources, and opportunities for minorities and others to enter the trucking industry; and protective regulation has resulted in some operating inefficiencies and some anticompetitive pricing.[12]

The intent of the MCA of 1980 is to give the ICC "explicit direction for regulation of the motor carrier industry and well-defined parameters within which it may act" in the interest of "the uncertainty felt by the nation's transportation industry."[13] In that same section, the Congressional mandate is clearly stated:

> The Interstate Commerce Commission should not attempt to go beyond the powers vested in it by the Interstate Commerce Act and other legislation enacted by Congress; and that legislative and resulting changes should be implemented with the least amount of disruption to the transportation system consistent with the scope of the reforms enacted.[14]

Entry Policy

Section 5 of the act establishes motor carrier entry policy. In many respects, it codifies the administrative changes made by the ICC prior to passage of the act. Congress rejected, however, a proposed "master certificate" approach previously adopted by the ICC, under which blanket approval would have been given to applications

---

[9] Motor Carrier Act of 1980, Pub.L. No. 96-296, section 4, 94 Stat. 793, 794 (1980).
[10] *Ibid.*
[11] *Ibid.*, section 3.
[12] *Ibid.*
[13] *Ibid.*
[14] *Ibid.*

meeting a standard of "public convenience and necessity . . . based upon general findings developed in rulemaking proceedings."[15] Thus, consideration of applications for authority continued on a case-by-case basis.

The provisions of section 5 ease barriers to entry in two ways. First, they ease the burden of proof of public convenience and necessity for those seeking new authority. Second, they constrain the possible scope of the basis of protest against applications for new authority. The language of section 5 retains the fitness test for entry, but substantially weakens the public need test. Specifically, the act directs the ICC to issue certificates to applicants for common carrier authority if it finds

> (A) that the person is fit, willing and able to provide the transportation to be authorized by the certificate and to comply with this subtitle and the regulations of the Commission; and (B) on the basis of evidence presented by persons supporting the issuance of the certificate, that the service proposed will serve a useful public purpose, responsive to a public demand or need; unless the Commission finds, on the basis of evidence presented by persons objecting to the issuance of a certificate, that the transportation to be authorized by the certificate is inconsistent with the public convenience and necessity.[16]

Applications for authority are still open to protest on the grounds of public convenience and necessity, but only by carriers that perform service within the scope of the proposed certificate, actively solicit that business, or have on file an application for that authority. The burden of proof with respect to public convenience and necessity under the statute falls on the protestor, not the applicant. In bearing that burden, a protestor is constrained by the statutory mandate that "the Commission shall not find diversion of revenue or traffic from an existing carrier to be in and of itself inconsistent with the public convenience and necessity."[17]

Operating Authority

Section 6 of the MCA deals directly with the "removal of certain restrictions on motor carrier operation."[18] In this section, Congress directs the ICC to "eliminate gateway restrictions and circuitous route limitations imposed upon motor common carriers of property

---

[15] *Ibid.*, section 5.
[16] *Ibid.*
[17] *Ibid.*
[18] *Ibid.*, section 6.

... [and] to process expeditiously applications ... seeking removal of operating restrictions" designed to

> (i) reasonably broaden the categories of property authorized by the carrier's certificate or permit;
> (ii) authorize transportation or service to intermediate points on the carrier's routes;
> (iii) provide round-trip authority where only one-way authority exists; and
> (iv) eliminate unreasonable or excessively narrow territorial limitations.[19]

The statute contains three additional provisions regarding operating restrictions. Section 6 authorizes carriers holding both common and contract authority to haul both types of cargo in the same truck at the same time. Section 9 of the act exempts "transportation of property by motor vehicle for compensation by a person who is a member of a corporate family for other members of such corporate family" from the jurisdiction of the ICC subject only to a notification requirement.[20] As a result, private carriers engaged in compensated intercorporate hauling among wholly owned subsidiaries are not subject to regulatory restrictions on entry or operation. Finally, section 10 specifies that in the case of a contract carrier "the Commission may not require such carrier to limit its operations to carriage for a particular industry or within a particular geographic area."[21]

Ratemaking

The MCA of 1980 is designed to both encourage and facilitate independent rate actions in several ways. Section 11 offers carriers the opportunity to raise or lower their rates within a "zone of rate freedom" without having to face the possibility that the ICC will exercise its power to "investigate, suspend, revise, or revoke any rate proposed by a motor common carrier."[22] The zone is set at 10 percent (plus or minus) over rates in effect one year prior to the effective date of the proposed rate change. The statute also provides for widening of the zone by administrative action within prescribed limits if the ICC finds that there are benefits to carriers, shippers, and the public "from further rate flexibility."[23] Section 12 of the act encourages rate innovation by allowing carriers to utilize released rates, which allow shippers to determine the value and cost

---

[19] *Ibid.*
[20] *Ibid.*, section 9.
[21] *Ibid.*, section 10.
[22] *Ibid.*, section 11.
[23] *Ibid.*

of the insurance they want on their cargo while in the hands of the carrier without prior ICC approval.

Section 14 of the act deals with the activities of rate bureaus. Rate bureaus were permitted to continue their previous activities until January 1, 1984, but were subject to statutorily imposed procedural requirements and limitations designed to restrict the rate bureaus' ability to discourage independent ratemaking and to disguise collective ratemaking. Rate bureaus "may not interfere with each carrier's right of independent action and may not change or cancel any rate established by independent action."[24] In addition, rate bureaus may not protest tariff changes proposed by individual carriers, and their employees may neither docket nor act upon the rate change proposals of individual members. Finally, with respect to collective ratemaking, bureau meetings must be open to the public and bureau records regarding proposals of, and votes on, rate changes must be made available on request.

The passage of the MCA effectively repealed the antitrust exemption for collective ratemaking with respect to single-line rates (rates for shipments not involving interlining between carriers from origin to destination) effective January 1, 1984. In addition, one of the provisions of the act stipulates the creation of a Motor Carrier Ratemaking Study Commission that must "make a full and complete investigation and study of the collective ratemaking process for all rates of motor common carriers and upon the need or lack of need for continued antitrust immunity therefor."[25]

THE IMPLEMENTATION OF THE ACT

ICC Chairman Darius Gaskins welcomed the Motor Carrier Act of 1980 as "one of the most significant accomplishments to date in reforming Federal regulation of our transportation economy."[26] At the same time, the ICC announced that it was

> ready and able to implement this legislation immediately. . . . We have developed a comprehensive program based on congressional policies easing entry into the trucking business to create a more competitive environment in the industry, giving rate flexibility to carriers acting individually, and reducing the trucking industry's anti-trust immunity.[27]

[24] *Ibid.*, section 14.
[25] *Ibid.*
[26] Interstate Commerce Commission, "ICC Chairman Unveils Implementation Plan for Truck Bill; Hails Legislation," *ICC News* (press release, July 2, 1980), p. 1.
[27] *Ibid.*

Entry

The passage of the MCA did not alter the ICC's established policy regarding the burden of proof with respect to the public interest in entry cases. In the opinion of the ICC's Office of Policy and Analysis, section 5 of the act "codified the change in burden of proof in entry applications thus permitting grants of authority not inconsistent with the public convenience and necessity [and] confirmed the general direction that Commission entry policy had recently taken and extended it by further reducing the importance of protecting existing carriers."[28]

The ICC issued "rules governing applications for operating authority" to "give effect to much of the new entry policy of the MCA, and establish procedural rules conforming to the statutory deadlines imposed by the legislation."[29] The effect of these rules and procedures, and the changed entry policy that they support on applications for authority, has been significant. The total number of applications for operating authority grew from 12,700 in 1979 (the year of administrative deregulation) to 22,735 in 1980 (the year of legislative deregulation) to over 29,000 in the twelve months following passage of the act.[30] Over the same period, grants of authority to new entrants increased from 690 in 1979 to 1,423 in 1980 and to 2,452 in the twelve months following passage of the act.[31] Two years after passage of the act, "applications appear[ed] to have leveled off ... at the rate of approximately 1,100 each month," but by that time 43,000 new certificates had been issued and almost 8,000 new carriers had been granted operating authority.[32]

The ICC also issued a policy statement on "acceptable forms of requests for operating authority" that, according to the ICC's Office of Policy and Analysis, "strongly encouraged carriers to apply for broad, unencumbered authority" in which "commodities should be defined in terms of generic commodity groups, and geographic territories should be at least countywide."[33] As a result of that policy,

---

[28] Interstate Commerce Commission, Office of Policy and Analysis, "The Effect of Regulatory Reform on the Trucking Industry: Structure, Conduct and Performance" (Washington, D.C.: ICC Office of Policy and Analysis, preliminary report, June 1981), p. 16.

[29] *Ibid.*, p. 17.

[30] Denis A. Breen, "Regulatory Reform and the Trucking Industry: An Evaluation of the Motor Carrier Act of 1980," statement submitted to the Motor Carrier Rate Making Commission, March 1982, p. 21 (transcript in author's possession).

[31] *Ibid.*

[32] Taylor, Statement on the Implementation of the Motor Carrier Act of 1980, p. 2.

[33] Interstate Commerce Commission, Office of Policy and Analysis, "Effect of Regulatory Reform," p. 17.

grants of authority in 1981 were far less encumbered by operating restrictions than they had been five years earlier.[34] In part, this development was as much administratively imposed as applicant requested, resulting in "numerous examples . . . of instances in which the Commission . . . gave an applicant much broader authority than the applicant even requested."[35] Also as a result of that policy, the ICC began to grant nationwide general commodity authority beginning in 1981 at the rate of about one per week.

The ICC's policy and practices on the scope of authority were challenged in court by the ATA. In October 1981 the U.S. Court of Appeals for the Fifth Circuit found for the ATA and against the ICC on the grounds that ICC expansion of authority beyond that requested by applicants was inconsistent with the requirement that a carrier be fit, willing, and able to provide the full service authorized.[36] Since then, the ICC has made some administrative adjustments in its operating policy, but has neither rescinded nor restricted its previously granted, overly broad operating authorities.

Operations

In "Elimination of Gateway Restrictions and Circuitous Route Limitations" the ICC issued rules to permit carriers previously authorized to provide through service to do so "over any available route."[37] At the same time, it issued "Removal of Restrictions from Authorities of Motor Carriers of Property," which established procedures and guidelines for carriers filing restriction-removal applications.[38]

The ICC began to accept restriction-removal applications in January 1981. By June of that year, approximately 2,700 applications had been received, all of which were approved as published in the *Federal Register*.[39] One year later, the number of such applications approached 5,000,[40] of which nearly all were approved as published

---

[34] *Ibid.*, pp. 49-52.

[35] Interstate Commerce Commission, "Position Paper of Chairman Reese H. Taylor," August 14, 1981, p. 9 (in author's possession).

[36] *American Trucking Ass'ns v. I.C.C.*, U.S.C.A. (5th Cir. 1981), No. 81-4026, October 1, 1981.

[37] "Elimination of Gateway Restrictions and Circuitous Route Limitations," 49 C.F.R. part 1042, Ex Parte No. MC-142. 45 *Federal Register* 86,741 (1980).

[38] "Removal of Restrictions from Authorities of Motor Carriers of Property," 49 C.F.R. parts 1002 and 1137, Ex Parte No. MC-142 (Sub-No. 1). 45 *Federal Register* 86,747 (1980).

[39] Breen, "Regulatory Reform and the Trucking Industry," p. 23.

[40] Taylor, Statement on the Implementation of the Motor Carrier Act of 1980, pp. 24-25.

in the *Federal Register*. The remaining few were approved with only slight modifications.

The commission issued a number of policy statements and rulings after passage of the act that lifted restrictions on the operating scope of various types of carriers, continuing a trend begun in the late 1970s. The ICC Office of Policy and Analysis stated that the first of these actions "removed all restrictions from the possession of both common and contract authority."[41] The second dealt with "Implementation of Intercorporate Hauling Reform Legislation" and the rules and requirements for qualifying for the compensated intercorporate hauling exemption from regulation. In related actions, the ICC also decided, according to the Office of Policy and Analysis, to permit private carriers to utilize owner-operators,[42] and proposed that private cariers be permitted "to trip lease their equipment and drivers to authorized carriers."[43] Finally, the commission eliminated regulation of any trailer-on-flatcar or container-on-flatcar service performed by railroads[44] and has proposed extending that exemption to include service by rail-affiliated motor carriers.[45]

The deregulation of private carriers engaged in compensated intercorporate hauling produced a visible, but not dramatic, response. By June 1981 a total of 648 parent corporations had submitted the required notice of intent to initiate compensated intercorporate hauling involving a total of 6,755 subsidiaries.[46] The effect of allowing private carriers to use owner-operators and to trip lease on the extent of private carriage remains to be seen, but the deregulation of motor-rail and rail-affiliated motor carriage has had an effect in the private sector similar to that observed in compensated intercorporate hauling.

The established trucking industry has not been sanguine about the ICC's policies regarding the character and scope of the compensated intercorporate hauling and trailer-on-flatcar/container-on-flatcar exemptions. The ATA challenged the ICC's determination that a private corporation could set up a wholly owned subsidiary

---

[41] Interstate Commerce Commission, Office of Policy and Analysis, "Effect of Regulatory Reform," p. 22.

[42] *Ibid.*, p. 23.

[43] "Leasing Rules Modifications," 49 C.F.R. part 1057, Ex Parte No. MC-43 (Sub-No. 12). 46 *Federal Register* 15,300 (1981).

[44] "Improvement of TOFC/COFC Regulation," 49 C.F.R. parts 1039, 1090, and 1300, Ex Parte No. 230 (Sub-No. 5). 46 *Federal Register* 14,348 (1981).

[45] "Improvement of TOFC/COFC Regulation, Railroad Affiliated Motor Carriers and Other Motor Carriers," 49 C.F.R. part 1039, Ex Parte No. 230 (Sub-No. 6). 46 *Federal Register* 14,365 (1981).

[46] Interstate Commerce Commission, Office of Policy and Analysis, "Effect of Regulatory Reform," p. 70.

engaged solely in transportation. It was unsuccessful in that challenge, a setback that in the ATA's view "significantly enhances the utilization of compensated intercorporate hauling and poses a serious threat to the continuation of a regulated transportation system in this country."[47] The ICC's decision to permit private carriers to use owner-operators has been characterized by the ATA as "another example of the I.C.C.'s undue efforts to expand private carriage,"[48] and has been challenged in the courts. The ATA also challenged the ICC's rail exemption, again without success. That setback, coupled with subsequent ICC actions, led the ATA to assert that "by its actions, the I.C.C. is removing the fastest growing segment of the transportation industry, TOFC [trailer-on-flatcar] service, from any regulatory controls." The ATA predicted that in so doing the ICC will be placing almost all TOFC service in the exclusive hands of the railroads,"[49] and the efforts of railroads to utilize deregulation to expand their motor carrier operations had led the ATA to argue that "safeguards against domination of one mode of transportation by another have become all the more necessary."[50]

Rates

The MCA of 1980 calls for procedural changes in the role of rate bureaus in the ratemaking process. The ICC rules to implement these mandated changes were issued in its ruling, "Motor Carrier Rate Bureaus—Implementation of Pub.L. 96-296," issued in December 1980. Among other reforms, these rules permit carriers to take independent rate actions without having to face the potential procedural obstacles posed by a rate bureau that has both the power to delay filing of a proposal with the ICC and the right to notify other members of the proposed action prior to its being docketed. The ICC's rules specifically provide that

> Rate Bureau agreements must provide each carrier the absolute right to decide whether or when an independent action, released rate, or rate within the zone of freedom, will be docketed. If independent actions are docketed they may not be discussed prior to the effective date of the tariff item.[51]

---

[47] Bennett C. Whitlock, Jr., Statement on Oversight—Motor Carrier Act of 1980 before the Surface Transportation Subcommittee, Committee on Public Works and Transportation, U.S. House of Representatives, June 23, 1982, Appendix I, p. 4 (Transcript in author's possession).

[48] *Ibid.*

[49] *Ibid.*, Appendix I, p. 8.

[50] *Ibid.*, Appendix I, p. 9.

[51] "Motor Carrier Rate Bureaus—Implementation of Pub.L. 96-296," 49 C.F.R. part 1331, Ex Parte No. 227 (Sub-No. 5). 45 *Federal Register* 86,736 (1980).

One effect of the above rule has been to permit carriers to file independent rate actions directly with the ICC, which statutorily has thirty days to review proposed actions. The commission, however, is empowered by statute to reduce the thirty-day notice period "if cause exists." Early evidence suggests that "a significant number of carriers" took advantage of their option to bypass rate bureaus in taking independent action.[52] Subsequent statements by the ATA suggest that in doing so they were greeted by an ICC disposed to act expeditiously on such action. Specifically, the ATA charged that

> although very few advance any argument at all that "cause exists," authority to make the tariff effective on 14 days' notice is routinely granted. One result of this, of course, is to cut in half the time for filing protests, which in turn makes the analysis of the tariff, the calculation of costs and revenues thereunder and the preparation and filing of a meaningful protest extremely difficult, and in many cases, impossible.[53]

The ICC's formal and informal administrative support of independent actions probably accounted, at least in part, for the fact that the number of independent rate filings approximately doubled from 1979 to 1980.[54] This trend continued in the following year, when the ICC reported that

> pricing innovation and independent ratemaking have continued to increase since enactment of the Act. In 1980, 60,600 independent rate actions were reported by major rate bureaus. In 1981, the figure increased to 115,085.[55]

The pricing innovations cited by the ICC have not gone unnoticed by the ATA, which has taken the position that

> since enactment of the Motor Carrier Act of 1980, extreme pressures have been exerted upon motor common carriers to engage in so-called "innovative" ratemaking. . . . [Such ratemaking] has taken a variety of forms, i.e., discounts predicated upon tonnage or revenue, flat percentage discounts, multiple shipments or aggregate tender discounts, and a raft of other variations of rates and charges.[56]

---

[52] Breen, "Regulatory Reform and the Trucking Industry," p. 24.

[53] Ross C. Gaussoin, Statement on Oversight—Motor Carrier Act of 1980 before the Surface Transportation Subcommittee, Committee on Public Works and Transportation, U.S. House of Representatives, June 23, 1982, p. 6 (transcript in author's possession).

[54] Marcus Alexis, Statement on Motor Carrier Act of 1980 before the Surface Transportation Subcommittee, Committee on Public Works and Transportation, U.S. House of Representatives, June 10, 1981, p. 3. (transcript in author's possession).

[55] Taylor, Statement on the Implementation of the Motor Carrier Act of 1980, p. 3.

[56] Gaussoin, Statement on Oversight—Motor Carrier Act of 1980, pp. 1-2.

The result of these practices, in the view of the ATA, has been "an unmistakable dismantling of the ratemaking system . . . that has for so many years been the cornerstone of the motor common carrier industry."[57]

The dismantling of the cornerstone of the industry was not accepted passively. In 1981, a group of common carriers banded together to form the Committee for Lawful Rates, which petitioned the ICC "to address the lawfulness of volume discount rates and aggregate tender rates."[58] The ICC addressed that question, but found no basis for action. This decision was characterized by the committee through the ATA as indicative of a virtual abdication of the ICC's rate regulatory authority, an abdication that

> was made complete when the Commission closed the door on the principal process through which it has always discharged its rate regulatory duties, namely, the suspension and/or investigation of rates. . . . It did so with the astonishing statement that "the suspension and investigation format is a premature process for addressing predation and that further standards aimed at that process would not be useful.[59]

THE IMPLICATIONS OF THE ACT

The MCA of 1980, as interpreted and implemented by the ICC, has weakened the regulatory foundation of trucking industry cartelization through its enhancement of the potential for both intermodal and intramodal competition. Deregulation weakened the structural soundness of the trucking industry cartel but in and of itself did not promise the quick or complete destruction of that cartel since it did not guarantee that the potential for increased competition would be quickly or fully realized. That problem was in large measure solved by the economic downturn of the early 1980s, which weakened the economic mortar of the cartelization of the industry: stable or growing demand. Thus, the combination of regulatory reform and declining demand have produced a rapid and extensive disintegration of the trucking industry cartel, with adverse effects on employment levels and carrier profits.

Barriers to Entry

The statutory and administrative changes in the scope and structure of the public need standard, coupled with the ICC's arguably

---

[57] *Ibid.*, p. 2.
[58] *Ibid.*, p. 3.
[59] *Ibid.*, pp. 4-5.

lax application of the fitness standard in granting new operating authorities, effectively has eliminated the major historical barriers to entry into the industry. Absent these barriers, entry into the industry is today relatively easy in terms of capital and manpower requirements, at least with respect to truckload freight. The terminal network required for the handling of less-than-truckload freight represents a substantial entry barrier, however, because of the financial and managerial resources it requires.

Statistics on the number and disposition of applications for new or extended operating rights provide only one measure of the implications of the relaxation of entry requirements. A far more significant measure of the economic implications of eased entry is the virtual elimination of the market for, and book value of, existing operating rights. The fact that such rights have become essentially valueless indicates that the discounted present value of future excess profits, which are attributable to and dependent upon restricted entry and the cartelization of the industry, is perceived as nonexistent.

Both the number and the disposition of applications for new or extended operating authority provide some indication of the capacity added to the industry since deregulation. The exact extent of additions to the capacity of the nation's for-hire motor freight transportation system is unknown, but it is clear that despite declining demand, new carriers were entering the industry and existing carriers were expanding operations at a substantial rate in the period immediately following deregulation. One explanation offered for such behavior is that carriers were "positioning themselves for competition in a less regulated environment even if this [meant] adding to capacity during a recession."[60]

Market Segmentation

Deregulation also served to weaken the elaborate set of barriers to competition among existing carriers that was created by regulatory limits on the extent of markets that individual carriers could serve. The ICC's efforts to avoid narrow restrictions on new operating authority and to eliminate such restrictions from existing operating authorities served to enhance the potential for competition among previously noncompetitive carriers. This was most evident in the case of common carriers, whose authorities typically carried geographic and/or commodity limitations, but also extended

---

[60] Breen, "Regulatory Reform and the Trucking Industry," p. 23.

to contract carriers, whose rights to serve multiple shippers and to act as both contract and common carriers traditionally had been limited. The ICC's policies on the regulation of private and rail motor carriage did the same for those two traditional noncompetitors.

Blurring the traditional competitive boundaries among common carriers and between common and other types of motor carriers is important in its own right since it creates a more competitive environment in the trucking industry. Combined with other ICC efforts to ease operating restrictions on the flexibility of all motor carriers, it produces a potential second incentive to enhanced competition: added capacity. The operating restrictions imposed on motor carriers of all types imply the existence of excess capacity in the industry to compensate for whatever inefficiency was occasioned by those restrictions. Thus, the elimination of those restrictions should free excess capacity for productive use, and thereby create a second source of increased supply as a consequence of deregulation. Unfortunately, there is no way to measure the magnitude of this effect of deregulation, but it must have been a crucial factor in the decision of the many established firms that added to capacity during a recession.

The efficiency/capacity effects of deregulation may be particularly significant in the private carriage sector of the industry. Operating restrictions imposed on private carriers prior to deregulation required them to operate with a substantially higher rate of empty miles than regulated carriers.[61] The proposed policies and rules of the ICC offer some hope of alleviating that problem, and may therefore provide a strong incentive for further expansion of such carriage, at the expense of for-hire carriage, through both new entry and expansion of existing operations. Whether deregulation will result in an "undue enhancement of private carriage" remains to be seen, but the historical record suggests it may not. In the 1950s a series of court decisions extended and then removed regulatory exemption for the transportation of frozen fruits and vegetables. Under deregulation, for-hire rates fell, as did the percentage of cargo hauled by private carriage; with reregulation, the reverse was the case.[62]

---

[61] Interstate Commerce Commission, Office of Policy and Analysis, "Effect of Regulatory Reform," p. 68.

[62] U.S. Department of Transportation, Office of Transportation Economic Analysis, "Effects of Deregulation on Less-Than-Truckload General Commodity Trucking," Contract No. DOT-OS-90028, January 1980, pp. 3-9–3-12.

Collective Ratemaking

The basic system of collective ratemaking was not altered substantially by the MCA of 1980 immediately following its implementation. The rate bureaus continued to operate and to seek and secure general rate increases to offset increases in operating costs. The *Wall Street Journal* estimated that trucking rates increased about 17 percent in the year following passage of the act.[63]

The combination of expanding capacity and stable or declining demand immediately following passage of the act created an environment more supportive of rate reductions than rate increases. The result was increased downward pressure on rates, to which carriers could respond either with improved service at existing rates or reduced rates for existing service. The former option was typically pursued under regulation and was chosen by some carriers under deregulation. By historical standards, a relatively large number of carriers discounted their rates after deregulation, which led to an increase in the number of independent actions from 27,141 in 1979 to 115,085 in 1981.[64] Most of these involved rate reductions or discounts, which were estimated by the *Wall Street Journal* to have reduced the 17 percent nominal increase in rates during the first year of deregulation to about 12 percent.[65]

The downward pressure on effective rates inevitably exerted downward pressure on profits and profitability. The extent of that pressure in 1980 was difficult to estimate, as return on equity for the industry in that year was clouded by extraordinary charges to income based on the loss in value of operating certificates. Rates of return on equity for large Class I carriers fell from 12.5 percent (excluding extraordinary charges) in 1980 to about 8.1 percent in 1981.[66]

The combination of deregulation and declining demand apparently eliminated so-called excess profits derived from cartelization and brought profits to more normal levels (with allowance for increased risk of failure). The ATA, however, has argued that conditions have driven profits for the industry as a whole substantially below that level.[67] This decrease in profits suggests the existence of

---

[63] John D. Williams, "Truck Deregulation Has Cut Rising Costs, Improved Service in a Year, Shippers Say," *Wall Street Journal*, June 30, 1981, p. 36.

[64] Taylor, Statement on the Implementation of the Motor Carrier Act of 1980, p. 10.

[65] Williams, "Truck Deregulation," p. 36.

[66] Taylor, Statement on the Implementation of the Motor Carrier Act of 1980, Appendix IV, p. 3.

[67] Whitlock, Statement on Oversight—Motor Carrier Act of 1980, p. 10.

excess capacity in the industry and also may indicate increasing pressure to leave the industry. By June 1981 it was "generally recognized by the Commission, the industry and the financial community that a shakeout [was] underway" as the effects of decreased demand eliminated marginal firms and the effects of increased competition eliminated inefficient firms.[68] This shakeout continued into 1982, when the ATA reported that 183 carriers had gone out of business and an additional 51 were experiencing financial difficulty.[69]

The economic problem confronting the industry is one of operating ratio. This ratio varied between 94 and 95 percent (with the exception of the recession year of 1975, when it exceeded 95 percent) under regulation in the 1970s and between 96 and 97 percent from 1978 to 1981.[70] The ATA views this as a product of the ICC's abdication of its traditional responsibility to regulate rates and rates of return, which indeed it is, because the commission is no longer willing to enforce a system of cost-plus pricing. In the absence of assured cost passthrough, carriers are subject to stronger incentives to control input costs, including negotiated factor price and usage, than was the case under protective regulation. Thus, management can no longer easily afford to "avoid or minimize confrontation with labor as well as the stern cost-cutting measures one frequently finds in unregulated industries."[71]

---

[68] Breen, "Regulatory Reform and the Trucking Industry," p. 29.

[69] Whitlock, Statement on Oversight—Motor Carrier Act of 1980, Appendix II, p. 1.

[70] *Ibid.*, Appendix III, p. 9.

[71] Milton Kafoglis, Statement on the Southern Motor Carriers Rate Conference, Inc., before the Interstate Commerce Commission, Investigation and Suspension Docket No. M-29772, July 5, 1978, p. 2.

CHAPTER VIII

The New Shape of the Trucking Industry

There is no dearth of articles, papers, statements, and studies on the effects of deregulation on the trucking industry. The consensus of these appraisals is that deregulation has had a definite impact on the performance, conduct, and structure of the industry. Beyond that, however, there is little agreement on the short-term extent and the long-term implications of the changes wrought by deregulation. Views expressed have ranged from warnings of a return to the self-destructive competition that necessitated regulation of the nation's transportation system in the 1930s to predictions of little more than a marginal intensification of preexisting trends.

There is general agreement that the trucking industry experienced what might be called a Great Shakeout in the three years following the passage of the Motor Carrier Act (MCA) of 1980. There is, however, no similar consensus on the extent to which that shakeout was attributable to deregulation of the industry rather than to the depressed demand confronting the industry during the same period. The MCA was signed into law at "the cyclical low point for intercity truck tonnage" and implemented during a period "when the economy continue[d] to be sluggish and the regulated trucking industry remained in a slump."[1] The fact that both depressed demand and deregulation usually encourage greater competition, with all of its consequences for resource allocation, raises a valid and difficult question regarding the share of blame or credit to be accorded to each factor in explaining the industry's shakeout.

Beyond the question of the immediate effects of deregulation is the broader issue of its long-term effects on the industry and on freight movement in general. To determine the long-term implications of recent events, extrapolation of the early effects of deregulation is unavoidable. In making such an extrapolation, two elements of regulatory reform play an important role: duration and degree. Opinions on the probable long-term impact of deregulation depend on the question of whether the shakeout was a product

---

[1] Denis A. Breen, "Regulatory Reform and the Trucking Industry: An Evaluation of the Motor Carrier Act of 1980," submitted to the Motor Carrier Ratemaking Study Commission, March 1982, p. 17 (in author's possession).

solely of the MCA or a product of the act and the two years of administrative deregulation that preceded it. Similarly, any determination of the potential impact of deregulation depends upon the extent to which it is recognized that deregulation, thus far, has been only partial, and that further deregulation, particularly in rate-making, lies ahead.

Those who maintain that the shape of the trucking industry today is the product of adaptation to five years of extensive deregulation, complicated and compounded at least temporarily by a cyclical recession, tend to assert that the worst is over and that the industry is once again poised to grow with the economy, albeit along a somewhat more competitive track.[2] Those who view the shape of the industry today as the embryonic stage of adaptation to a still new and partial deregulation assert that the worst is yet to come, that the industry faces a further, more fundamental economic and institutional transformation that will make it a less viable and valuable component in the nation's transportation system.[3] The truth undoubtedly lies between these two extremes, but in any event, the path toward equilibrium is not likely to be easy for the established carriers and their union workers, for whom the news during recent years "has been mostly dreary."[4]

THE AFTERMATH OF DEREGULATION

The dreary news for the industry began with the 1980 recession and lasted through 1983. The recession initiated a downward trend in the volume of intercity motor freight traffic that continued through 1982, by which time volume had fallen by almost 15 percent from its 1979 level (see Table VIII-1). The drop in demand for intercity trucking service was accompanied by a decline in nonsupervisory employment in the trucking industry of about 7.5 percent between 1979 and 1981 (Table VIII-1). The more limited extent and duration of the decline in employment relative to the decline in volume must be attributed to the fact that the employment data include both local and intercity trucking while the volume data are limited to intercity trucking.

---

[2] See, for example, U.S. General Accounting Office, *Effects of Regulatory Reform on Unemployment in the Trucking Industry* CED-82-90 (Gaithersburg, MD: U.S. General Accounting Office, June 11, 1982).

[3] See, for example, Irwin H. Silberman, Statement Before the Subcommittee on Surface Transportation, Committee on Commerce, Science and Transportation, U.S. Senate, September 21, 1983.

[4] Agis Salpukas, "Trucking's Great Shakeout," *New York Times*, December 13, 1983, p. D-1.

TABLE VIII-1

Trucking Industry Volume and Employment
1979–1984

Year	Intercity Ton Miles (Billions)		Nonsupervisory Employment (Thousands)	
	number	percent change	number	percent change
1979	608	—	1,105.7	—
1980	555	−8.7	1,044.0	−5.6
1981	527	−5.0	1,020.5	−2.3
1982	520	−1.3	1,120.8	+9.8
1983	548	+5.4	1,132.5	+1.0
1984	602	+9.9	1,211.6	+7.0

Sources: Transportation Policy Associates, *Supplements, Updates and Corrections to Transportation in America* (Washington, D.C.: Transportation Policy Associates, November 1985) p. 6; and U.S. Department of Labor, Bureau of Labor Statistics, *Employment, Hours, and Earnings, United States, 1909–84,* March 1985, Volume II, p. 646.

The declining demand for intercity trucking service particularly affected carriers of general freight. These carriers experienced approximately a 15 percent drop in tonnage between 1979 and 1980 and another 15 percent drop between 1980 and 1983.[5] The fact that general freight carriers represented the most heavily unionized segment of the industry was clearly reflected in the impact of declining demand on the employment of members of the International Brotherhood of Teamsters (IBT) in the trucking industry. The industry unemployment rate rose from approximately 6 percent in 1979 to 12 percent in early 1981 before falling to under 9 percent by early 1982.[6] The Teamsters, however, estimated that between 19 and 24 percent of its trucking industry members were unemployed in early 1981[7] and subsequently stated that

> the regulated general freight industry has suffered severe decreases in profits and employment since the enactment of the Motor Carrier Act of 1980. The major causes of the financial losses and high unemployment are both the economic recession and the Motor Carrier Act of 1980. We have not been able to separate the effects of each

---

[5] Silberman, "Statement Before the Subcommittee on Surface Transportation," p. 9.

[6] U.S. General Accounting Office, *Effects of Regulatory Reform,* p. 4.

[7] Norman A. Weintraub, "Layoffs and Unemployment, April 1981, Motor Carriers of General Freight and the Regulated Trucking Industry: Survey of 37 Representative Local Unions Under the National Master Freight Agreement and Chicago Trucking Agreements" (International Brotherhood of Teamsters, final report, July 29, 1981), p. 4 (in author's possession).

major cause but the combined impact is extremely significant, between 26% and 32% on layoff in April, 1982.[8]

The decreases in profits and financial losses cited by the Teamsters were real and substantial. Between 1979 and 1982, the operating ratios of general freight carriers increased from about 96 percent to almost 99 percent, according to the results of one study of 249 such carriers,[9] and it was reported that in 1982 "fully 40% of all regulated carriers had net losses."[10] From the viewpoint of the American Trucking Associations (ATA), one consequence of such adverse trends in operating ratios and profitability was the demise of an unusually large number of trucking firms. An ATA study conducted in mid-1982 indicated that

> 188 ICC regulated motor carriers have now apparently closed their doors and gone out-of-business ... [and] another 49 ICC regulated firms are currently experiencing financial difficulties—ranging from voluntary curtailment of service to reorganization under Chapter 11 of the Federal Bankruptcy laws.[11]

THE RESPONSE TO DEREGULATION

There is no way and no need to attempt to accurately allocate blame for the woes of general freight carriers and the Teamsters between recession and deregulation. It is, however, possible and productive to trace the response of those inside and outside the industry to the opportunities afforded by deregulation in an effort to identify emergent changes in the economic structure of trucking activity. The two types of opportunity afforded by deregulation are entry (routes) and pricing (rates). The sources of information regarding response to those opportunities include, in addition to the aforementioned press and other reports on deregulation, data on aggregate regulatory activity drawn from government reports and on individual carrier activity drawn from the IRU questionnaire conducted as part of this study.

---

[8] Norman A. Weintraub, "Comments and Analysis of U.S. General Accounting Office, *Effects of Regulatory Reform on Unemployment in the Trucking Industry*" (International Brotherhood of Teamsters, June 21, 1982), p. 1 (in author's possession).

[9] Silberman, Statement Before the Subcommittee on Surface Transportation, p. 4.

[10] Nelson J. Cooney, "How Deregulation Has Changed Industry," *Transport Topics*, November 28, 1983, p. 4.

[11] Richard A. Staley to Bennett C. Whitlock, Jr., "Analysis of Motor Carriers That Have Gone Out-of-Business Since Mid-1980 (6th Update)—Revised," internal memorandum of August 4, 1982, American Trucking Associations, Inc., p. 1 (in author's possession).

Entry

The primary thrust of deregulation was to ease requirements for entry into the regulated trucking industry. The result, despite the depressed state of demand for trucking service in 1980 and 1981, was a continuation of the upward trend in requests for new operating authority that had begun under administrative deregulation. Approximately 30,000 requests were received in the twelve months following passage of the MCA of 1980. Since then, the number of applications for new operating authority has not changed dramatically; the character of these applications changed, however, as more new entrants, as opposed to existing carriers, began to request new operating authority.

Restructuring Existing Authorities. Deregulation eased the barriers facing existing firms in rationalizing and/or restructuring their routes in the interest of greater efficiency. The act encouraged carriers to seek the removal of restrictions on existing operating authority, which many, including two-thirds of the common carriers responding to the IRU questionnaire, were quick to do. Deregulation also enabled firms to seek new authority to compliment existing authority in an effort to enhance their competitive position. Again, many regulated carriers, including almost 90 percent of such carriers responding to the IRU questionnaire, were quick to avail themselves of this opportunity. Thus, most of the applications for new operating authority in the year following deregulation were filed by existing carriers.

The responses of regulated carriers to the IRU questionnaire suggest that requests for new operating authority by existing carriers often involved extension of service into regions not served prior to deregulation. At the same time, however, some firms were terminating or curtailing service in regions previously served, although on a far more limited scale. Thus, one response to deregulation appears to have been an expansion of the geographic scope of operations by many existing common carriers and a regional realignment of operations by a few others. Changes in the scope and structure of operations were accompanied by both the opening and closing of terminal facilities among the carriers responding to the IRU questionnaire. Among these carriers, more reported opening new terminals than closing old ones and on a larger scale in the case of openings than closings. Such actions are clearly consistent with the finding that

> despite a sluggish economy, carriers are expanding operations into newly acquired territories. Equipment is being reassigned and terminals are being added to carrier networks. . . . Carriers seem to be

positioning themselves for competition in a less regulated environment even if this means adding capacity during a recession.[12]

New Entrants. The second and third years after passage of the MCA of 1980 produced a growing number of applications for operating authority from new entrants to the industry who obviously believed that despite the sluggish economy the industry offered them adequate long-term profit opportunity. As a result, the total number of regulated carriers increased from 18,000 in June 1981 to 22,000 in June 1982, and to 30,000 in June 1983. The additions to the industry population were primarily small carriers, as evidenced by the fact that more than 90 percent of the approximately 4,000 regulated carriers added to the industry between June 1981 and June 1982 had operating revenues of less than $1 million.[13] The entrants typically were not only small, but also tended "to concentrate, at least initially, on truckload business (either general or special commodities) where capital requirements and administrative skills are less."[14] That pattern had not changed by 1983, when it was observed that although

> reduced economic regulation ha[d] increased competitors and resulted in sharply lower truckload volumes to the full-service general commodity carriers, it ha[d] apparently not introduced substantial new competitors nor dramatically affected volumes of the LTL business, where substantial capital investment is required of new entrants.[15]

Two types of new entrants into the truckload freight market deserve particular attention. The first is comprised of the railroads and other transportation companies. Technically, such companies are not newcomers to the trucking industry, since many were involved previously in regulated trucking activity in conjunction with their primary services. The scope of such operations, however, was severely restricted by regulation. Deregulation has permitted these carriers to rid themselves of such restrictions and to capitalize on the advantages of containerized freight. As a result,

> the new breed of transportation companies are "multimodal" or "fully integrated." Their "intermodal" service is "cradle to grave," also known as "total transportation."[16]

The second type of new entrant is comprised of companies that technically are not new entrants to the industry and statistically

---

[12] Breen, "Regulatory Reform and the Trucking Industry," p. 22.
[13] U.S. General Accounting Office, *Effects of Regulatory Reform,* p. 6.
[14] Breen, "Regulatory Reform and the Trucking Industry," p. 22.
[15] Silberman, Statement Before the Subcommittee on Surface Transportation, p. 11.
[16] Bill Paul, "Moving It," *Wall Street Journal,* October 20, 1983, p. 1.

are not even part of the industry: private carriers. Deregulation eased many of the barriers to cost-effective private carriage and created the option for private carriers to engage in compensated intercorporate hauling. The results of the IRU questionnaire suggest that a number of established private carriers, like common carriers, acted fairly quickly to avail themselves of the opportunities afforded by deregulation. Approximately 40 percent of the responding private carriers reported that they had taken advantage of their option to seek supplemental operating authority to act as regulated common or contract carriers. Fully one-third of the respondents reported that they had filed the documents required to permit them to engage in compensated intercorporate hauling, placing themselves among the more than 900 companies that had signed up to do so among an estimated 10,000 wholly owned subsidiaries by the end of 1983.[17]

Pricing

The combination of depressed demand caused by the recession, and increased capacity, a result of deregulation, produced an intensification of competition within the industry. Deregulation paved the way for price competition to an extent far beyond that permitted under regulation. The result, according to 96 percent of the regulated carriers and 92 percent of the private carriers responding to the IRU questionnaire, was an unprecedented amount of rate discounting by for-hire carriers following passage of the MCA of 1980.

The most intense price competition in the early 1980s was in the truckload segment of the freight market, in which "freight rates collapsed as the industry exploded with new entrants after it was deregulated in 1980."[18] The primary beneficiaries of the collapse in freight rates were the large shippers of truckload freight, particularly those large enough to exercise a sufficient degree of monopsonistic power to put them in the driver's seat when negotiating rates with the exploding population of small, truckload-lot carriers.[19] Potentially included among such shippers were a number of large private carriers, many of whom apparently found that rate discounting reduced or eliminated the cost advantages of private carriage. One-quarter of the private carriers responding to the IRU questionnaire indicated that their private carriage operations had been curtailed or, in a few cases, eliminated after 1980; more than

---

[17] Cooney, "How Deregulation Has Changed Industry," p. 3.

[18] Agis Salpukas, "A 2-Tiered Trucking System," *New York Times*, March 29, 1984, p. D-1.

[19] See, for more detailed discussion, "Shippers Are in the Driver's Seat," *Business Week*, October 18, 1982, pp. 182-86.

half of those carriers attributed their situation primarily to deregulation.

The less-than-truckload segment of the industry did not witness the explosion of new entrants experienced by the truckload segment after deregulation. It did experience, however, a substantial increase in the total number of firms as a result of the aforementioned efforts of existing carriers to position themselves for competition in a less regulated environment. These efforts added to the excess capacity created in the less-than-truckload market by the recession and the removal of operating restrictions under deregulation. The inevitable result was growing competition manifested primarily in a host of creative pricing or discounting practices.

THE INDUSTRY AFTER DEREGULATION

Deregulation altered the basic shape of the regulated trucking industry in two ways. First and foremost, it served to divide the industry into two economically and technologically distinct segments—less-than-truckload and truckload freight. That dichotomy within the industry existed long before deregulation, but had been repressed by regulation and, to a lesser extent, by collective bargaining. Second, it served to bring price competition to both segments of the industry. The potential for such competition also existed prior to deregulation, but again had been suppressed and/ or redirected by regulation and, to a lesser extent, by collective bargaining.

Bifurcation

Truckload and less-than-truckload carriers serve two distinct markets for motor freight transport and operate with two different sets of capital and operating costs. Truckload carriers are low-cost/ low-service providers of motor freight carriage to shippers needing point-to-point service for large lots of freight. Less-than-truckload carriers are high-cost/high-service providers of motor freight service to shippers requiring point-to-point carriage of small lots of freight. In theory, those two types of freight carriage should be characterized by two sets of prices fully reflective of the differences in the costs of the services provided. In fact, that does not appear to have been the case prior to deregulation because: 1) most large regulated carriers operated in both markets; and 2) these carriers charged differential rates in the two markets that did not fully reflect differences in cost of service, resulting in the overpricing of truckload and underpricing of less-than-truckload haulage.

It is difficult to prove directly that truckload rates were too high and less-than-truckload rates too low in relation to the costs of those two types of service, but it is not hard to do so indirectly. The fact that deregulation resulted in a flood of new entrants into the truckload market in relation to the level of new entrants into the less-than-truckload market clearly suggests that those outside the industry perceived the existence of above-normal profit opportunities in that market. These new entrants to the truckload market could afford to undercut existing rates with rates more closely aligned to the cost of service and still earn at least a normal profit. If they did, it would be at the expense of the truckload operations of established general freight carriers. That, indeed, appears to have been the case, as evidenced by the conclusion of one study of the tonnage losses of a sample of general freight carriers that

> the post-1979 decline in less-than-truckload (LTL) activity was modest ... [while] truckload activity of the general freight carriers declined by almost one-quarter in 1980, and exhibited a further sharp decline in 1982.[20]

The loss of truckload tonnage, as expected, was reported in the same study to have "had a disproportionate effect on general freight carrier profitability."[21] That effect was particularly pronounced because "the major decline in TL activity of the full-service carriers occurred in the so-called class-rated TL traffic, the rates for which are generally intended to recover fully distributed costs."[22] The loss of lucrative class-rated truckload business eliminated its subsidy of the costs of the less-than-truckload business of full-service carriers, forcing these carriers to pass on to less-than-truckload shippers "the additional costs which have been thrust upon the general freight motor carriers because of the loss of truckload business."[23] The resulting full costing of less-than-truckload service is one factor accounting for the fact that while truckload rates in 1983 were 5 percent below their 1980 level, less-than-truckload rates were 20 percent higher.[24]

Competition

The growing competition for truckload freight forced established general freight carriers either to become competitive in that market

---

[20] Silberman, Statement Before the Subcommittee on Surface Transportation, p. 9 (emphasis in original).

[21] *Ibid.*, p. 12.

[22] *Ibid.*

[23] *Ibid.*, p. 13.

[24] "Deregulating America," *Business Week*, November 28, 1983, p. 86.

or to abandon it and concentrate their attention and resources on the less-than-truckload market. The former option required substantial cost cutting and efficiency improvement; the latter, substantial capital investment and strategic planning. Firms that could not do either were forced to leave or to attempt to leave the industry.

The most formidable barrier facing many firms in striving to become competitive in the truckload market was the need to gain adequate and timely relief from existing contractual obligations and restrictions under the NMFA and related agreements. As has been indicated, the Teamsters were not, as a matter of policy, unreceptive to the possibility of such relief. The question facing the parties at the local level often was not whether concessions would be made, but whether they could be made in time to save a carrier. In one such case, the carrier was quoted as follows:

> They [the competition] cut rates so fast and drastically that even if you were in negotiations with your union you couldn't get the new lower rates in, since by then they had already cut your price. I just decided to get out.[25]

The option pursued by this carrier and by many large unionized general freight carriers was to concentrate on the less-than-truckload market. The keys to success in pursuing that strategy were flexibility and financing. In that context, nonunion status was an advantage, but not a prerequisite for success, judging by two of the early success stories in the industry: Overnite Transportation and Roadway Express. Overnite, a nonunion firm, gained an early advantage in the scramble for less-than-truckload business by offering an across-the-board 10 percent discount to less-than-truckload customers. In the view of *Forbes*, its "current industry advantage stems directly from Overnite's nonunion status. Because unionized companies were stuck with high labor costs, many couldn't hold rates without heading into the red."[26] Roadway, on the other hand, was a unionized carrier depicted by *Forbes* as able to achieve a comparable level of control within the confines of labor agreements because it recognized that "labor costs amount to roughly two-thirds of Roadway's revenues, so the ability to control them is crucial."[27] In both cases, however, *Forbes* also noted the absence of debt as an important source of competitive strength, which was compounded in the case of Roadway by "a $305 million cash hoard that can finance new terminals and equipment or a rate-cutting grab for market share."[28]

---

[25] Salpukas, "A 2-Tiered Trucking System," p. D-1.
[26] Jay Gissen, "No Union Dues, No Union Blues," *Forbes*, October 12, 1981, p. 219.
[27] Jean A. Briggs, "Easing into High Gear," *Forbes*, August 31, 1981, p. 92.
[28] *Ibid.*, pp. 91-92.

Clearly, not all established general freight carriers were in as favorable a position as Overnite or Roadway to consolidate and enhance their position in an increasingly competitive less-than-truckload market, and many carriers that lacked the flexibility and financing necessary to operate profitably in the market were forced out of the industry. Yet because the Multiemployer Pension Plan amendments to the Employee Retirement Income Security Act make participating employers in such plans liable for the full amount of their share of the unfunded liability of the plan at the time of withdrawal from it, some unionized carriers "limp along losing money but unwilling to liquidate, because that could mean handing over their assets to the pension funds."[29] As Ronald Roth, director of statistical research for the ATA, has observed, "while there is now open entry into trucking, there is no open exit."[30]

---

[29] Charles G. Burck, "Deregulation Gets a Yellow Flag from the ICC," *Fortune*, September 7, 1981, p. 86.

[30] Lawrence Minard, "Truckers and Shippers," *Forbes*, January 2, 1984, p. 108.

CHAPTER IX

The New Shape of Trucking Labor Relations

The fundamental labor relations question arising out of deregulation is the extent to which it will alter the long-term economic viability of unionized carriers and/or the long-term institutional viability of the union bargaining system. It is still too early to seek a definitive answer to that question, because the industry and its industrial relations system have just begun the process of settling into a new long-term competitive equilibrium. It is not too early, however, to begin the search for the answer to that question by examining the short-term impact of deregulation on union presence and influence within the industry and on its problems and performance at the bargaining table.

UNION PRESENCE

The common carrier respondents to the Industrial Research Unit's questionnaire of common and private carriers strongly believed that there had been an increase in the extent of open shop competition since deregulation. Seventy percent of those respondents "strongly agreed" that such a trend existed, and another 20 percent "agreed" that this had been the case. Eighty percent of the respondents expressing such a view also "agreed" that the increase in open shop competition was "primarily" the result of deregulation.

The views of the responding common carriers on the trend of union influence in the industry after deregulation were not as definitive. Only 35 percent indicated a strong belief that union influence had decreased, and although another 40 percent agreed that union influence had waned, almost 25 percent saw no such trend. The logical explanation for this difference in the perceived trends of union presence and union influence is that most new entrants to the industry after deregulation were small truckload-lot carriers, which caused rapid growth in open shop competition in that market. If large, less-than-truckload-lot carriers, which have been the heart of the International Brotherhood of Teamsters' (IBT) influence in the industry, had experienced such growth, perceptions would certainly have been different.

Small Carriers

It seems highly unlikely that the influx of new entrants to the ranks of the industry's smaller carriers has not significantly changed the union/nonunion balance among such carriers. There are, however, no available quantitative data to measure the extent, if any, of such change. Class III carriers that were exempt from most Interstate Commerce Commission (ICC) reporting require- ments prior to deregulation continued to be exempt after deregu- lation. A substantial portion of the 2,000 Class II carriers not exempted from such requirements in 1979 were exempted in 1980 by virtue of an increase in the revenue limit between Class III and II. Finally, other exemptions from either regulation or reporting requirements for various types of carriers substantially reduced the number of Class II carriers reporting operating data to the ICC. Overall, those changes resulted in a drop in the number of Class II carriers reporting complete operating data to the ICC from 2,000 in 1979 to 100 in 1982.[1]

The change in the size limits of Class II carriers in 1980 was largely responsible for a drop in the number of such carriers filing operating reports with the ICC from 2,043 to 290. Those 290 carriers were about equally divided between union and nonunion carriers, as judged by the presence or absence of reported contributions to health and welfare/pension funds. Union carriers were slightly larger and seemingly more productive than nonunion carriers, with average employment of sixty-two workers and average operating revenue per worker of $49,950, as compared with average employ- ment of sixty workers and average operating revenue per worker of $49,675 for their nonunion counterparts.

By 1981, the number of reporting Class II carriers had dropped to about 130. These 130 carriers were again divided almost equally between union and nonunion, as determined by the presence or absence of reported contributions to health and welfare/pension funds. In 1981, unlike 1980, nonunion carriers were slightly larger and substantially more productive than union carriers, with average employment of fifty-one workers and average operating revenue per worker of $87,650, as compared with average employment of fifty workers and average revenue per worker of $77,050 for their union counterparts.

The ICC data for those Class II carriers required to report oper- ating data in 1980 and 1981 provide a basis for calculating average

---

[1] Unless otherwise noted, all data presented in this chapter are derived from the Interstate Commerce Commission's databank of trucking industry statistics.

annual wage, benefit, and total compensation costs per employee for both union and nonunion carriers. Although these calculations provide only a very crude measure of relative compensation costs, they do suggest the existence of a substantial and growing union/ nonunion differential at the time of, and immediately following, deregulation (see Table IX-1). These calculations also tend to confirm that the greatest relative compensation advantage of nonunion over union carriers is in the area of benefits rather than wages.

The growing compensation cost differential between union and nonunion Class II carriers between 1980 and 1981 is hardly surprising given the existence of multi-year union-management contracts in the union segment of the industry, which inevitably slow the process of adapting to new economic conditions. The same effect may also have been at work in the differential rate of change of operating revenue per employee between union and nonunion firms between 1980 and 1981. This pseudomeasure of labor productivity showed a dramatic rise for both union and nonunion carriers between 1980 and 1981 as a result of the economic and regulatory forces that reduced the number of reporting Class II carriers from 290 to 130. There was, however, a clear difference in the rate of change between union and nonunion carriers, which served to enhance further the compensation cost and labor cost advantages of nonunion carriers (see Table IX-2).

The most recent year for which ICC data are (or may ever be) available for Class II carriers is 1982. In that year none of the 114 Class II carriers—representing only 4,900 workers—who filed reports on their operations reported any contribution to health and

TABLE IX-1

Average Annual Compensation Costs
Union and Nonunion Carriers
Class II: 1980 and 1981
(per employee)

	1980			1981		
Compensation	Union	Nonunion	Union as Percentage of Nonunion	Union	Nonunion	Union as Percentage of Nonunion
Wages	$21,295	$20,011	106	$23,132	$21,308	109
Benefits	2,796	2,072	135	2,973	1,513	196
Total	24,091	22,083	109	26,105	22,821	114

Source: ICC databank of trucking industry statistics.

TABLE IX-2

*Average Annual Operating Revenues
and Compensation Costs
Union and Nonunion Carriers
Class II: 1980 and 1981*
(per employee)

	Union			Nonunion		
	1980	1981	Percent Change	1980	1981	Percent Change
Operating Revenues	$49,955	$77,046	+54	$49,674	$87,666	+76
Compensation Costs	24,091	26,105	+ 8	22,083	23,821	+ 3
Ratio of Operating Revenues to Compensation Costs	2.07	2.95	+42.5	2.25	3.84	+70.7

Source: ICC databank of trucking industry statistics.

welfare/pension funds. Although this clearly cannot be interpreted to mean that the Teamsters no longer have any presence or influence among Class II carriers, it does suggest that the Teamsters' benefit and/or bargaining systems are frail and failing even among this group of medium-sized carriers.

Large Carriers

Class I carriers were the core of Teamster presence and influence in the industry prior to deregulation. In 1979, 95 percent of all such carriers were unionized, based on reported contributions to benefit funds, as compared to less than 20 percent of all Class II carriers. Not all of these unionized Class I carriers were completely organized, as indicated by the fact that their average contribution per employee to benefit funds was only 73 percent of that required by the National Master Freight Agreement (NMFA), rather than an expected value of 87 percent (the percentage of all employees in the industry who are production workers). Much of the discrepancy can be attributed to some forty lightly unionized carriers that contributed less than $1,000 per employee per year to benefit funds.

In marked contrast to developments in the three years of administrative deregulation preceding passage of the act (see Table IX-3), the three years following passage of the Motor Carrier Act (MCA) of 1980 produced not only a decline in the total number of Class I carriers but also some changes in the composition of those carriers. The most obvious change was the tripling, in both absolute and

TABLE IX-3

Class I Carriers Classified by
Benefit Fund Contributions
1979–1983

Year	Total Carriers (number)	Heavily Unionized (number)	Heavily Unionized (percent of total)	Lightly Unionized (number)	Lightly Unionized (percent of total)	Nonunion (number)	Nonunion (percent of total)
1977	321	272	85	36	11	13	4
1978	329	271	82	39	12	19	6
1979	332	275	83	41	12	16	5
1980	308	252	82	35	11	21	7
1981	272	222	82	34	12	16	6
1982	276	204	74	37	13	35	13
1983	288	195	68	45	16	48	16

Source: ICC databank of trucking industry statistics.

relative terms, of the number of nonunion carriers. A second, more subtle change was the relative growth of lightly unionized carriers vis-à-vis all unionized carriers, which contributed to, but does not completely explain, the drop between 1979 and 1983 in average annual contribution per employee to benefit funds by unionized carriers from 73 to 60 percent of the NMFA-required amount.

The significant numerical growth of nonunion and lightly union ized Class I carriers between 1979 and 1983 overstates the extent of their presence in the industry. Although such carriers represented almost one-third of all Class I carriers in 1983, they accounted for less than one-sixth of the total employment and revenues of these carriers. Thus, in 1983 the average employment of heavily unionized carriers was over 1,500, as compared to 750 for lightly unionized carriers and 200 for nonunion carriers.

The small average employment size of nonunion Class I carriers relative to their unionized counterparts suggests the possibility that they may be little more than small fish in a big pond. Yet such a characterization, however appropriate in specific segments of the industry, overlooks the very real competitive advantages of nonunion carriers in the area of labor cost, as revealed by operating data submitted to the ICC. Such data indicate the existence of a sizable and growing gap between the pay and productivity of workers of union and nonunion Class I carriers in the early 1980s sufficient to make nonunion carriers a potential competitive threat beyond the weight of their numbers and market share (see Table IX-4). Such data also indicate that lightly unionized carriers occupy

TABLE IX-4

*Average Annual Compensation
and Revenue Per Employee
Union and Nonunion Class I Carriers
1979 and 1983*

	1979		Union	1983		Union
	Union	Nonunion	Nonunion	Union	Nonunion	Nonunion
Wages	$22,366	$16,842	1.33	$27,293	$18,630	1.46
Benefits	2,907	1,057	2.75	4,096	897	4.57
Total Compensation	25,273	17,899	1.41	31,389	19,527	1.61
Operating Revenue	45,336	53,720	.84	52,555	81,097	.65
Ratio of Operating Revenues to Compensation Costs	1.79	3.00	.60	1.67	4.15	.40

Source: ICC databank of trucking industry statistics.

a middle ground in all competitive battlefields between union and nonunion Class I carriers (see Table IX-5).

The fact that nonunion Class I carriers were able to generate two and one-half times more operating revenue per compensation dollar than their unionized counterparts in 1983 lends strong support to the view of the 87 percent of the respondents to the IRU questionnaire who agreed that "open shop status is by itself a significant competitive advantage in the trucking industry." The competitive advantage of open shop carriers resulted equally from lower pay and higher productivity. The most dramatic difference between the

TABLE IX-5

*Average Annual Pay and Productivity
Per Employee for Class I Carriers
by Extent of Unionization
1983*

		Lightly		Union	Lightly Unionized
	Union	Unionized	Nonunion	Nonunion	Nonunion
Wages	$27,293	$21,734	$18,630	1.46	1.17
Benefits	4,096	1,365	897	4.57	1.52
Compensation	31,389	23,099	19,527	1.61	1.18
Revenue	52,555	57,219	81,097	.65	.70
Ratio of Revenue to Compensation	1.67	2.48	4.15	.40	.60

Source: ICC databank of trucking industry statistics.

two types of carriers is in the area of benefit costs, where the average annual cost per employee for nonunion firms was only about one-fifth of that for unionized firms. In general, the same pattern of operating differences also characterized lightly unionized carriers, but at a much lower level.

COLLECTIVE BARGAINING

The more broadly based policies of adjustment to growing non-union competition that were not conceded by the Teamsters in 1979 were finally accepted in 1982. The most obvious difference between 1982 and 1979 in the circumstances surrounding NMFA negotiations was the 26 to 32 percent layoff rate of employees of regulated general freight carriers in April 1982. A more subtle and more important difference was the fact that by 1982 the Teamsters' loss of organizational control over the industry had advanced so far that the union could no longer ignore the threat of nonunion competition without fear of a further loss of union jobs.

The 1982 NMFA

The growing price competition fostered by the combination of recession and deregulation in the early 1980s forced most established carriers to undertake cost-control and cost-cutting programs. Since labor costs account for almost two-thirds of total cost in regulated trucking, the result was strong and growing pressure during the term of the 1979 NMFA to put labor back into competition. By 1982, pressure was being felt not only by smaller (short haul) carriers but also by the larger (long haul) carriers, who for the most part had been spared the rigors of competition prior to deregulation. Since the larger carriers effectively controlled the industry's NMFA bargaining agent, Trucking Management Incorporated (TMI), accommodation to labor competition assumed an importance on the industry's bargaining agenda in 1982 that it had not commanded in 1979.

Both the union and the industry approached the 1982 NMFA negotiations hoping for an agreement that would enable them to strengthen their relative positions in the increasingly competitive world of trucking. The two parties eventually settled on an agreement that did not adversely affect their respective positions. The agreement contained no obvious union concessions, in marked contrast to the trend of the times, but it did contain several implicit concessions that became manifest only during the term of the agreement and that provided the wage restraint required to avoid a further widening of union-nonunion wage/benefit differentials.

The 1982 NMFA provided for no general wage increases and called for no major benefit changes during its term. It did call, however, for the payment of the $0.72 cost of living adjustment (COLA) due April 1, 1982 (allocating $0.47 to wages and $0.25 to benefits) and for the continuation of COLA under the existing formula. COLA increases under the new agreement were to be given annually rather than semiannually. In addition, the agreement provided for the possible diversion of some or all COLA increases to fund the costs of existing benefits should the parties agree on such action at the time the increases were payable, as they did in both 1983 and 1984.[2]

The 1982 NMFA clearly did not threaten to weaken the competitive position of large, unionized general freight carriers vis-à-vis their nonunion counterparts. It did not and could not, however, do much to improve the competitive position of large, unionized carriers with respect to labor cost. That matter was left to be addressed in regional negotiations over supplements to the NMFA. The result was a set of subtle but significant changes in work rules through which progress was made toward phasing out the terminal-to-terminal rule—a rule that, according to the *Wall Street Journal*, "protects the jobs of more than half of the drivers and warehouse workers covered by the agreement."[3]

The 1982 NMFA may have met the immediate competitive needs of the large unionized carriers of general freight, but it was too little and too late for a large number of small unionized carriers, particularly those attempting to survive in the highly competitive truckload market. Such carriers had no choice but to attempt to divorce themselves from the national negotiations and agreement and to seek local negotiations and agreements in which their individual competitive conditions could be discussed and accommodated. The result was a further proliferation of the under-the-table arrangements of the 1970s, to the point where they were more a rule than an exception among small and/or truckload carriers.

The basic focus for such local negotiations was the possibility of economic givebacks. There are no data on the extent of such givebacks, but it can be noted that more than 50 percent of the unionized common carriers responding to the IRU survey reported that they had received concessions. The most prevalent area of concession

---

[2] Bureau of National Affairs, *Daily Labor Report* No. 58 (March 26, 1984), p. A-6.
[3] "Teamster Aides Reach Tentative Accord with Truckers That Would Phase Out a Costly Work Rule," *Wall Street Journal*, December 18, 1981, p. 4.

was wage reduction or suspension of wage increases, but concessions were also reported in pay for time not worked and premium pay (see Table IX-6). As *Business Week* observed at the time, "because the industry has decided that 'you don't mess with' pension or health benefits . . . wages and paid time off are the primary areas for cutting costs."[4]

The combination of the reasonable 1982 NMFA settlement and the resumption of economic growth halted, but did not reverse, the downward trend in Teamster employment in the trucking industry. Under the pressure of continuing high unemployment rates among Teamster members (or former members) in trucking, the union entered into talks with TMI in mid-1983 to search for a solution to the stagnant employment situation in the unionized sector of the industry. The result of these talks was a tentative agreement on a national rider to the NMFA that proposed to "cut wages and benefits by up to 31% for laid-off and newly hired trucking industry workers" in an effort to "make Teamsters' wages more competitive with those of nonunion truckers."[5] This tentative agreement on a two-tier wage system was submitted to the union's trucking membership for a ratification vote in September 1983 and was overwhelmingly rejected, 94,000 to 13,000

The defeat of the 1983 rider was a stinging political setback for the Teamsters' leadership. The Teamsters for a Democratic Union (TDU) characterized the rider, as they had the 1982 NMFA, as a sweetheart deal and saw in its rejection a vindication of TDU's position that "people are getting tired of these concessions" and that "the hierarchy of our union has grown out of touch with the

TABLE IX-6

Reported Union Concessions

Form of Concession	Percentage of Union Firms
Reduction or Suspension of Wages	52
Reduction of Vacations or Holidays	24
Reduction of Overtime Modification	20
Reduction or Elimination of Daily Guarantees	15
Reduction or Elimination of Weekly Guarantees	11

Source: Industrial Research Unit questionnaire, 1983.

---

[4] "What the Teamsters' Pact Won't Do," *Business Week*, February 1, 1982, pp. 17-18.

[5] " 'A Real Slap in the Face' for Jackie Presser," *Business Week*, October 3, 1983, p. 43.

members."[6] The real reason for the rejection was probably better stated by *Business Week*, which attributed it to the fact that "workers were upset that the cuts were so pervasive, [and] saw that if [they] had been implemented, then in 1985 the industry would have tried to cut their wages."[7]

Overall, the 1982 NMFA increased hourly wage rates from $12.74 to $13.21, or by only 3.7 percent over its term. That increase fell short of the 5.3 percent increase in average hourly earnings in trucking between 1981 and 1984, resulting in a slight narrowing of the NMFA-industry wage differential. The narrowing of that differential, however, was more illusory than real because it was primarily the result of the diversion of COLA to benefit costs. Because of these diversions, the hourly cost of employer contributions to the two benefit funds increased from $2.2625 to $3.1925, or by more than 41 percent, between 1981 and 1984. The result was an increase in total hourly compensation costs of about $1.40, or 9.3 percent, during the term of the 1982 NMFA.

The 1985 NMFA(s)

The competitive fragmentation of the regulated trucking industry, which had threatened to undermine industrywide bargaining as early as 1977, had by 1985 progressed to the point that even the Teamsters with all of their power and pragmatism could not hold the system together. As a result, the union's 1985 master freight negotiations involved bargaining with three sets of carriers: Trucking Management Incorporated (TMI); Motor Carriers Labor Advisory Committee (MCLAC); and Regional Carriers Incorporated (RCI). According to published reports, TMI represented "35 of the nation's largest trucking companies employing approximately 90,000 active employees," MCLAC bargained for "about 115 firms employing between 40,000 and 50,000," and RCI represented carriers employing "about 20,000 workers."[8]

The IBT-TMI negotiations clearly were the center ring of the three-ring circus of trucking negotiations in 1985. The large national carriers still represented by TMI in 1985 had weathered the storm of deregulation and succeeded in rationalizing and restructuring their operations to meet the challenge of a more competitive market environment that, in the case of large carriers, was not primarily a product of new entry and nonunion competition. Thus, those car-

---

[6] Winston Williams, "Dissidents Charge a 'Sellout' On Teamster Contract Talks," *New York Times*, December 18, 1981, p. A-20.

[7] " 'A Real Slap in the Face,'" p. 43.

[8] Bureau of National Affairs, *Daily Labor Report* No. 63 (April 2, 1985), p. A-11.

riers were a logical and possibly easy target for the union's basic economic demands, which included the first general wage increases to be granted since 1982. The large national carriers agreed to an increase of $0.50 per hour in each year of the contract, and to an increase of $0.10 per hour ($4 per week) in employer contributions to the benefit funds. The agreement was not universally well received by smaller carriers, however; it was reported that "many MCLAC employers are unhappy with the settlement, feeling there should have been cost reductions rather than pay raises."[9]

The carriers that had broken away from TMI and had joined MCLAC in order to avoid domination by the large national carriers were not able to escape that domination in 1985 with respect to wages and benefits. MCLAC accepted an economic settlement identical to that of TMI, and won only limited recognition of the special circumstances of its constituents in the form of "a separate grievance procedure, separate committees, and a separate contract supplement." The fate of carriers represented by RCI is unknown, since it failed to reach an agreement with the union. Instead, it disbanded, leaving its members, like other independents, to cut their own deals.

The 1985 TMI agreement contained two notable new features. The first was a system of wage discounting for new hires. Under that system, new hires would receive 80 percent of the applicable contract rate in their first year, 80 percent in their second year, and 90 percent in their third year. In addition, the union agreed to cut the hourly wages of casual workers from $13.00 to $11.00 per hour. These two concessions prompted the expected TDU criticism of the settlement, but did not seriously jeopardize its ultimate ratification, largely because both affected groups (new hires and casual workers) were for the most part not eligible to vote on ratification.

The second notable new element in the 1985 TMI agreement was contract language designed to halt the de-unionization of carrier operations through doublebreasting and other means. The 1985 agreement declared null and void "all existing or previously adopted Riders which provide less than the wages, hours and working conditions specifically established by this Agreement." In addition, it provided that "corporate reorganizations by a Signatory Employer, occurring during the term of this Agreement, shall not relieve the Signatory Employer of the obligations of this Agreement during its term." Finally, the agreement added the following language to the provisions regarding work preservation:

> In addition, the Signatory Employer agrees that it will not, as hereinafter set forth, subcontract or divert the work presently performed

---

[9] *Ibid.*, pp. A-11–A-12.

by, or hereafter assigned to, its Employees to other business entities owned and/or controlled by the Signatory Employer, or its parent, subsidiaries or affiliates.[10]

It is too early to predict what the consequences of the 1985 NMFA will be for the industry and the union. The agreement will raise union hourly wages and compensation costs by about 11 percent over its term, and although such increases are quite modest by historical standards, it remains to be seen how they will compare to the trends in wage and benefit costs of nonunion carriers in coming years. The effect that the discounting of new hire wage rates will have on the unemployment rate of NMFA Teamster members also remains to be seen. In 1985, Teamster unemployment may have been as high as 20 percent, judging by a difference of 40,000 between the reported 200,000 employees covered by the agreements negotiated in 1985 and the 160,000 active employees of the carriers involved in the negotiations.[11] Finally, it is too early to tell what effect the union's contractual efforts to stop doublebreasting will have on the de-organization of the trucking industry, but judging by what has happened to the coverage of the NMFA, it seems likely that those efforts will be too little and too late. Depending on whether one assumes a Teamster coverage of 200,000 or 160,000 truckers in 1985, union coverage declined by either 17 or 34 percent between 1982 and 1985, bringing the total decline in coverage since 1970 to between 100,000 and 140,000 members, or between 33 and 50 percent (see Table IX-7).

TABLE IX-7

Workers Covered by the NMFA
1970–1985

| Date of Agreement | Teamster Membership | Decrease | |
		Number	Percent
1970	306,037	—	—
1973	297,833	8,204	2.7
1976	283,366	14,467	4.9
1979	277,017	6,349	2.2
1982	242,909	34,108	12.3
1985-High	200,000	42,909	17.7
1985-Low	160,000	82,909	34.1

Source: 1970-1983, data from U.S. General Accounting Office; 1985, data from Bureau of National Affairs.

---

[10] Bureau of National Affairs, *Daily Labor Report* No. 97 (May 20, 1985), p. E-11 (italics omitted).

[11] See Bureau of National Affairs, *Daily Labor Report* No. 63 (April 2, 1985), p. A-11.

CHAPTER X

Conclusion

The character of the trucking industry changed radically between 1964 and 1984. In 1964, the industry was a model of stability and order under the powerful but benevolent control of its two regulatory masters—the Interstate Commerce Commission (ICC) and the International Brotherhood of Teamsters (IBT). In 1984, however, the industry appeared to be a model of instability and chaos under the control of neither of its former masters.

At first glance, the culprits responsible for the loss of union organizing power in the trucking industry are deregulation and the Motor Carrier Act (MCA) of 1980. Yet although there can be little doubt that deregulation has had a profound effect on the state of the trucking industry, deregulation may well have been only the immediate, rather than the underlying, cause of the ensuing turmoil. There is substantial evidence that the loss of union organizing power in the industry began, and had made substantial progress, long before the advent of deregulation. The key to that process was the gradual erosion of the IBT's organizational control over the industry during the 1970s.

Deregulation opened the industry to entry and price competition, both of which have become widespread since the passage of the MCA in 1980. Such competition suggests that individuals perceived an opportunity under the MCA to make at least normal profits in the industry by charging less than prevailing rates, and expected to be able to operate on lower long-term cost curves than those traditionally prevalent in the industry. Since labor costs account for about 65 percent of total cost, such expectations would have to be predicated largely on the assumption of lower labor costs; and in the trucking industry, any expectation of lower labor costs must be predicated on the assumption that organization by the Teamsters and/or adherence to the terms of the Teamsters' NMFA and related contracts can be avoided. In 1964, such an expectation was not reasonable, but in 1984 it was, because the IBT was no longer the organizational threat that it was when it had relatively free access to secondary boycott pressure as an organizing technique.

The IBT's loss of economic organizing power in the industry was not immediately accompanied by a parallel loss in economic bargaining power over the unionized segment of the industry. Yet as changing political conditions within the union after the departure of Jimmy Hoffa forced the union to use its power more aggressively in its NMFA and related negotiations, the result was a series of economic settlements during the 1970s that created a substantial real and/or potential labor cost differential between union and nonunion carriers. This differential encouraged the expansion of nonunion (non-NMFA) operators even prior to deregulation, as evidenced by the spread of special commodity riders (geographically and by commodity) and special arrangements during the 1970s.

The result of these special riders and arrangements was the growing implicit recognition of a basic dichotomy in the trucking industry between special commodities and general freight. This institutional dichotomy paralleled, albeit imperfectly, a much more basic economic dichotomy within the industry between truckload and less-than-truckload freight: economically, the two types of freight were differentiated by the greater overhead cost (terminals) required to handle less-than-truckload freight; institutionally, the two types were differentiated by the greater degree of direct union control over less-than-truckload freight operations in terms of both wages and work rules.

The immediate effect of deregulation was to make explicit the previously implicit economic distinction between truckload and less-than-truckload freight. A secondary effect of deregulation was to emphasize and greatly expand the previously hidden institutional distinction between the truckload and less-than-truckload segments of the over-the-road freight market. In both cases, deregulation brought to light the actual and/or potential competitive role of nontrucking firms and their non-Teamster (or non-NMFA) employees in the over-the-road movement of freight, particularly truckload freight.

THE ECONOMICS OF THE INDUSTRY

The trucking industry after deregulation has become two distinct industries, each operating on a different long-term cost curve and each quite different in terms of services, technologies, and entry requirements. The first and lower-priced industry is truckload lot motor freight; the second and higher-priced is less-than-truckload lot motor freight.

Truckload Lot Industry

The truckload motor freight industry is characterized by ease of entry. The capital and skill requirements of truckload operation are limited, and as a result this sector of the industry has seen the greatest influx of new entrants since the passage of the MCA of 1980. Thus, it is not surprising that the truckload industry today is comprised of a relatively large number of smaller firms, many of which are new, and is characterized by relatively strong price competition for the business of truckload lot shippers, as evidenced by the drop in truckload freight rates between 1980 and 1983. Not surprisingly, this segment is dominated by "nonunion companies . . . which have a low overhead and rely on drivers who own their own trucks to haul the freight, [and] that have become a potent force in the trucking industry."[1]

Private carriers have also been increasingly active in the truckload market over the past two decades. The MCA of 1980 opened the door for further expansion of private carrier activity, but it also created a competitive climate within the truckload segment of the trucking industry that may make expansion of private carriage uneconomic. One reaction of large shippers to growing competition in the truckload market has been to concentrate their traffic volume in the hands of fewer common carriers in order to gain more bargaining leverage over rates, thereby reducing the cost advantage of private carriage. For example, Sears reduced the number of common carriers it utilized from 4,200 in 1980 to 210 in 1983, and indicated that its ultimate goal was to reduce that number to approximately 160.[2]

The railroads constitute a third participant in the truckload freight market. The MCA of 1980, as implemented by the ICC, allowed railroads, as well as private carriers, greater freedom of operation in the truckload market. The Staggers Rail Act confirmed and extended the competitive latitude of the railroads, which produced the potential for stronger intermodal competition in the truckload market. As a result, "railroads are going after new business . . . that went only to trucks in the first place because the rails were so tangled in regulation."[3]

---

[1] Agis Salpukas, "A Nonunion Trucker's Rise," *The New York Times*, March 16, 1982, p. D-1.

[2] Nelson J. Cooney, "How Deregulation Has Changed Industry," *Transport Topics*, November 28, 1983, p. 4.

[3] "A Painful Transition for the Transport Industry," *Business Week*, November 28, 1983, p. 86.

Less-Than-Truckload Lot Industry

The less-than-truckload motor freight industry, unlike the truck-load segment of the industry, is characterized by substantial capital and skill barriers to entry. A less-than-truckload operation "isn't just a trucking company; it's a distribution network,"[4] and as such, less-than-truckload haulage is not an option for those "fledgling motor carriers [who] can buy a few trucks and start serving bulk customers" but who can't profitably develop a nationwide distri-bution network.[5] As a result, the less-than-truckload market is pop-ulated primarily by large, established firms, most of which have been driven from the competitive chaos of the deregulated truckload market to the still relatively sheltered less-than-truckload market.

The less-than-truckload market has higher rates than the truck-load market because it is more labor intensive.[6] This does not nec-essarily mean that less-than-truckload freight is more profitable, as opposed to more expensive, than truckload freight; indeed, quite the opposite appears to be the case, judging by the increases in less-than-truckload freight rates that are allegedly a necessary conse-quence of the loss of truckload business by general freight carriers. Rate increases have brought less-than-truckload freight rates to a level where they reflect the full cost of handling such freight, the result of which has been to afford a competitive advantage to those firms with the lowest labor cost in the most labor-intensive segment of a generally labor-intensive industry. The primary beneficiaries from this situation thus far have been such nonunion firms as Overnite Transportation, whose "current industry advantage stems directly from [its] nonunion status."[7]

The mass migration of established trucking firms from the truck-load to the less-than-truckload segment of the industry, which was prompted by the massive influx of new entrants into the truckload market following passage of the MCA of 1980, has produced over-crowding and overcapacity in both segments. The result inevitably will be a further shakeout of the weak and inefficient firms in both industries, and given the labor-intensive character of trucking, the first victims of this shakeout are likely to be those firms that cannot control and reduce their labor costs. Carriers organized by the Teamsters and covered by the union's NMFA and related agree-

---

[4] Jean A. Briggs, "Easing into High Gear," *Forbes*, August 31, 1981, p. 92.
[5] *Ibid.*
[6] Aaron Bernstein, "Carolina Pacific?" *Forbes*, June 20, 1983, p. 58.
[7] Jay Gissen, "No Union Dues, No Union Blues," *Forbes*, October 12, 1981, p. 220.

ments face the greatest institutional barriers in meeting the challenge, since the contract system and the traditionally flexible and pragmatic union that controls it cannot supply unlimited flexibility and pragmatism, as the rejection of the proposed 1983 National Rider to the NMFA proved. The question now facing the union and its bargaining partners in the industry is whether they can stretch the NMFA to encompass two distinct and dissimilar segments of the trucking industry: truckload and less-than-truckload.

THE LABOR RELATIONS OF THE INDUSTRY

In 1964 the Teamsters were close to achieving the goal of taking trucking industry labor out of competition. The trucking industry was heavily unionized, and nonunion competition was slight. Bargaining in the trucking industry was centralized and the terms and conditions of employment effectively had been standardized. By 1984, however, labor in the trucking industry was once again largely back in competition, chiefly as a consequence of deregulation. The industry was no longer almost totally organized, and nonunion competition had greatly increased. Bargaining remained centralized, but the national industry standards had been substantially undermined by the myriad local and regional arrangements required by unionized trucking firms to cope with the new competitive reality.

Truckload Lot Industry

The truckload segment of the trucking industry in 1984 was basically nonunion. The IBT's organizational hold on truckload trucking was tenuous even before deregulation, as evidenced by the special commodity rider system, and its hold was further weakened by the new entry that followed deregulation. Union control of any sort may be totally broken by recent court decisions denying the union the right to impose contractual conditions on the right of unionized carriers to use owner-operators as independent contractors.[8] The IBT can seek to regain organizational control in truckload trucking by organizing the owner-operators on which most firms rely heavily, but the prospects for success in such an effort appear dim at best, judging by the historical record and current legal constraints on organizing tactics.

---

[8] See, for example, Building Material and Dump Truck Drivers, Teamsters Local Union No. 36 v. NLRB, 669 F.2d 759 (1981).

Less-Than-Truckload Lot Industry

The less-than-truckload segment of the trucking industry was still basically unionized in 1984, but the unions' hold continued to be threatened by serious and growing nonunion competition. New competition constituted a threat sufficient to force the union to accept a change in its long-standing terminal-to-terminal rule, and competition is likely to continue as a source of pressure in NMFA negotiations. The traditional economic pragmatism of the IBT leadership suggests that further compromises may be reached, but the mounting political turmoil within the union, as manifested most recently in the rejection of the 1983 two-tier rider to the NMFA, suggests that compromises may in fact be delayed, particularly since the union still holds an obvious short-term bargaining power advantage over less-than-truckload unionized carriers.

The Teamsters' best defense against nonunion competition would be an organizing offensive among nonunion less-than-truckload carriers. Numerically, such a task would appear far more manageable than organizing the truckload industry, but institutionally, the limits on secondary boycott activity and the fact that nonunion employers can match union wages and benefits at potentially lower cost because they are not participants in multiemployer benefit plans would probably defeat any Teamster attempt in this area. Thus, although it seems highly unlikely that the Teamsters will be driven from the less-than-truckload market given the requirements for entry, it also appears that the IBT will not easily drive nonunion competition from the market. If this is indeed the case, the union will continue to face the paradoxical situation of having to compromise because of its lack of organizing power while it still enjoys the considerable strength of its advantage in bargaining power.

THE FUTURE OF DEREGULATED TRUCKING

The combined forces of deregulation and depression in the trucking industry have accentuated and accelerated two long-term trends attributable to a decline in the organizing (as opposed to bargaining) power of the IBT within the industry. The first trend is the union's shrinking organizational control over truckload trucking, a situation that after deregulation left the union largely confined to the less-than-truckload market. This isolation within the more technically complex segment of the industry in turn accentuated the second trend: the decline, in both relative and absolute terms, of Teamster freight membership to the point at which it now constitutes only 9 percent of total Teamster membership. Politically, this

10 percent is very important within the union; economically, it is not. Thus, it is not surprising that the union leadership has publicly stated that freight is still a top union priority.[9] Privately, however, one must wonder how important freight will be in the future of what is probably the nation's largest and most diverse union. No union can easily shed its roots, and it therefore seems likely that the IBT will fight valiantly to hold on to the territory it now has. At the same time, it seems unlikely that the Teamsters will expend substantial resources to secure and expand its traditional territory given other and possibly easier organizational frontiers unless the union determines that its access to new frontiers is directly dependent on its record in trucking. If this is the case, the IBT will be forced to solve its organizing problems within the trucking industry in order to alleviate any appearance of weakness—a difficult task without easy access to secondary boycott pressure.

If the IBT can continue to make compromises in bargaining without being labelled weak, it should be able to maintain both its precarious hold in the truckload market and its powerful hold on the less-than-truckload market. If it cannot do so, however, the union will almost inevitably be driven from the less-than-truckload segment of the industry. The scenario that ultimately unfolds depends upon the relative power of pragmatism versus politics as the determinant of union policy in the 1980s and beyond. Should politics prevail, it may well be that the Teamsters will follow the same path to organizational erosion and isolation in the trucking industry that the United Mine Workers followed in the coal industry.

---

[9] "G.P. Presser Says: Of IBT's Highest Priorities, Freight's #1," *The International Teamster*, June 1984, p. 14.

APPENDIX

Deregulation and Open Shop Trucking Questionnaire

For office use only

☐ ☐ ☐ ☐

Part One—Your Firm

What is your firm's name and complete corporate address? (If anonymity is desired, please enter your zip code in the boxes below for statistical purposes.)

_____

_____

_____

1   ☐ ☐ ☐ ☐ ☐

Please indicate in the boxes the ICC codes that describe your firm.

2   ☐ Class: A. Class I   B. Class II   C. Class III
    ☐ Performance Code: A. Common   B. Contract Carrier
    ☐ Commodity Code: A. Gen. Freight   B. Special Commodities
    ☐ Service Code: A. Regular Route   B. Irregular Route

Please check the industry trade organization(s) of which your firm is a member. (Multiple response permitted.)

3   ☐ A. ATA
    ☐ B. ATA State Organization
    ☐ C. Regular Route Common Carrier Conference
    ☐ D. Irregular Route Common Carrier Conference
    ☐ E. National Tank Truck Carrier Conference
    ☐ F. Other ATA Conference
    ☐ G. Other Trade Association(s)

Please indicate in the boxes the number of years your firm has been in business.

4   ☐ ☐ ☐ years.   For example: five years = ☐ ☐ ⑤ years

Please check the appropriate box to indicate whether your firm initiated or filed any independent rate actions before or after January 1, 1980.   Y. Yes   N. No

5   Ⓨ Ⓝ Before January 1, 1980.
    Ⓨ Ⓝ After January 1, 1980.

Please check the appropriate box to indicate whether your firm offered a rate discount program before or after January 1, 1980.   Y. Yes   N. No

6   Ⓨ Ⓝ Before
    Ⓨ Ⓝ After

If your firm is a general freight carrier, did (do) these rate discounts apply to LTL traffic?   Y. Yes   N. No

7   Ⓨ Ⓝ Discounts offered before January 1, 1980.
    Ⓨ Ⓝ Discounts offered after January 1, 1980.

Please check the appropriate box to indicate whether your firm has applied to the ICC for the removal of restrictions from its operating authority or for additional authority.   Y. Yes   N. No

8   Ⓨ Ⓝ Removal of restrictions.
    Ⓨ Ⓝ Additional authority.

Please enter in the appropriate boxes your firm's total operating revenues in 1981, or your last fiscal year, to the nearest million.

9   $☐ ☐ ☐ ☐ million.   For example: $10 million = $ ☐ ☐ ① ⓪ million

Please check the appropriate box(es) to indicate the ICC region(s) in which your firm operated before January 1, 1978. (Multiple response permitted.)

    1. New England   2. Middle Atlantic   3. East North Central
    4. S. Atlantic   5. W. North Central   6. West Central
    7. W. South Central   8. Mountain   9. Pacific

10   ① ② ③ ④ ⑤ ⑥ ⑦ ⑧ ⑨

Please check the appropriate box(es) to indicate the ICC region(s) in which or into which your firm has expanded since January 1, 1978. (Please refer to the regions listed in question 10; multiple response permitted.)

11   ☐1 ☐2 ☐3 ☐4 ☐5 ☐6 ☐7 ☐8 ☐9

Please check the appropriate box(es) to indicate the ICC region(s) in which your firm has ceased or reduced operations since January 1, 1978. (Please refer to the regions listed in question 10; multiple response permitted.)

12   ☐1 ☐2 ☐3 ☐4 ☐5 ☐6 ☐7 ☐8 ☐9

Please enter in the boxes the number of your firm's terminals that furnish intercity service.

13   ☐ ☐ ☐ terminals provide intercity service.

Please enter in the boxes the percentage of these terminals that are subject to union agreements.

14   ☐ ☐ ☐ percent of the intercity terminals are subject to union agreements.
For example: ☐ 7 5 percent

Excluding replacements, please indicate the number of new terminals that your firm has opened and the number of old terminals that have been closed since January 1, 1978.

15   ☐ ☐ ☐ terminals were opened since January 1, 1978.
    ☐ ☐ ☐ terminals were closed since January 1, 1978.

Excluding replacements, please enter in the boxes the percentage of the opened terminals which are union and the closed terminals which were union.

16   ☐ ☐ ☐ percent of the terminals which were opened since January 1, 1978 are union.
    ☐ ☐ ☐ percent of the terminals which were closed since January 1, 1978 were union.

Please indicate the percentage of your firm's total nonsupervisory operating work force that is represented by a union. (This includes drivers and helpers; vehicle maintenance and repair personnel; cargo handlers; and clerical and administrative personnel.)

17   ☐ ☐ ☐ percent are represented by a union.

Please indicate the approximate percentage of nonsupervisory operating workers in each classification who are represented by a union:

18   ☐ ☐ ☐ percent of the firm's drivers and helpers are represented by a union.
19   ☐ ☐ ☐ percent of the firm's vehicle maintenance and repair personnel are represented by a union.
20   ☐ ☐ ☐ percent of the firm's cargo handlers are represented by a union.
21   ☐ ☐ ☐ percent of the firm's clerical and administrative personnel are represented by a union.

Please indicate the nature of the predominate union representation.   A. Teamster   B. Machinist
C. Steelworker   D. Other union with national affiliation   E. Independent union with no national affiliation
F. No union representation

22   ☐A ☐B ☐C ☐D ☐E ☐F   Drivers and Helpers
    ☐A ☐B ☐C ☐D ☐E ☐F   Vehicle Maintenance
    ☐A ☐B ☐C ☐D ☐E ☐F   Cargo Handlers
    ☐A ☐B ☐C ☐D ☐E ☐F   Clerical and Administrative

If your firm is signatory to a labor agreement with an independent union, are the wages and benefits:
A. less than,   B. equal to,   C. or greater than the wages and benefits provided by the relevant Teamster agreement in your area?

23   ☐A ☐B ☐C

If you are a union firm, have you established nonunion and/or double breasted operations since January 1, 1978? Did you attempt to do so before January 1, 1978?

24   ☐Y ☐N   Before January 1, 1978.
25   ☐Y ☐N   After January 1, 1978.

If your firm has union operations, please indicate if it has received any of the following union concessions.
Y. Yes   N. No

26   ☐Y ☐N   Wage Reductions or Suspensions of Increases
    ☐Y ☐N   Overtime Modifications or Reductions
    ☐Y ☐N   Daily Guarantee Reductions
    ☐Y ☐N   Weekly Guarantee Reductions
    ☐Y ☐N   Vacation or Holiday Reductions

Part Two—Your Competition

Does your company compete directly with carriers employing open shop trucking operations?   Y. Yes   N. No

27   ☑ Y   ☑ N

If so, please check the appropriate box to indicate when this competition began.

28   ☐ A. Before the mid-1970s
     ☐ B. Between 1975 and the passage of the MCA of 1980
     ☐ C. After the passage of the MCA of 1980
     ☐ D. All of the above
     ☐ E. Both A & B
     ☐ F. Both A & C
     ☐ G. Both B & C

Would you agree that since the late 1970s there has been an increase in the amount of open shop competition in the intercity trucking industry?
A. Strongly Agree   B. Agree   C. No Opinion   D. Disagree   E. Strongly Disagree

29   ☐ A   ☐ B   ☐ C   ☐ D   ☐ E

Would you agree that since the late 1970s there has been a decrease in the level of union influence on the intercity trucking industry?
A. Strongly Agree   B. Agree   C. No Opinion   D. Disagree   E. Strongly Disagree

30   ☐ A   ☐ B   ☐ C   ☐ D   ☐ E

If you are a union, general freight carrier, what percentage of your firm's truckload business would you estimate has been lost to open shop carriage since the late 1970s?

31   ☐ ☐ ☐ percent.

Would you agree that the lost truckload business was primarily backhaul traffic?
A. Strongly Agree   B. Agree   C. No Opinion   D. Disagree   E. Strongly Disagree

32   ☐ A   ☐ B   ☐ C   ☐ D   ☐ E

If you are a union special commodity or contract carrier, what percentage of your firm's business would you estimate has been lost to open shop carriage since the late 1970s?

33   ☐ ☐ ☐ percent.

Would you agree that open shop status is by itself a significant competitive advantage in the trucking industry? Would you agree that being organized by a union other than the Teamsters is often a significant competitive advantage?
A. Strongly Agree   B. Agree   C. No Opinion   D. Disagree   E. Strongly Disagree

34   ☐ A   ☐ B   ☐ C   ☐ D   ☐ E   Open shop status
     ☐ A   ☐ B   ☐ C   ☐ D   ☐ E   Unionized, but not by the Teamsters

If your firm has open shop operations, would you agree that your firm has taken active measures to oppose or resist unionization in these operations?
A. Strongly Agree   B. Agree   C. No Opinion   D. Disagree   E. Strongly Disagree

35   ☐ A   ☐ B   ☐ C   ☐ D   ☐ E

Would you agree that any increase in open shop activity in this industry is primarily the result of "deregulation" (which would include the actions of the ICC during the late 1970s)? Or, would you agree that any such increase is primarily due to the union carriers' higher rates, and would have occurred without "deregulation"?
A. Strongly Agree   B. Agree   C. No Opinion   D. Disagree   E. Strongly Disagree

36   ☐ A   ☐ B   ☐ C   ☐ D   ☐ E   The increase in open shop activity is primarily the result of deregulation.
     ☐ A   ☐ B   ☐ C   ☐ D   ☐ E   The increase in open shop activity would have occurred without "deregulation."

Would you agree that an unprecedented amount of rate discounting has occurred within the industry since mid-1980?
A. Strongly Agree   B. Agree   C. No Opinion   D. Disagree   E. Strongly Disagree

37   ☐ A   ☐ B   ☐ C   ☐ D   ☐ E

Part Three—Labor Market Activities

Please check the appropriate box to indicate how often you use each of the following methods to hire new workers.

A. Always   B. Often   C. Occasionally   D. Never

38 [A] [B] [C] [D] Ask current employees for recommendation
    [A] [B] [C] [D] Ask other employers to recommend someone
    [A] [B] [C] [D] Contact workers your firm employed in the past
    [A] [B] [C] [D] Contact union for reference
    [A] [B] [C] [D] Run a newspaper ad
    [A] [B] [C] [D] Contact workers who previously applied for a job
    [A] [B] [C] [D] Use the state employment service
    [A] [B] [C] [D] Contact a local vocational or training school

If your firm has open shop operations, please indicate the percentage of your nonsupervisory operating personnel (drivers, drivers' helpers, vehicle maintenance, cargo handlers, clerical and administrative) in these operations who were once (or are currently) union members.

39 [ ] [ ] [ ] percent were once or are currently union members.

Please check the appropriate box to indicate how often your firm utilizes the following pre-employment screening techniques.

A. Always   B. Often   C. Occasionally   D. Never

40 [A] [B] [C] [D] Written Application
    [A] [B] [C] [D] Interview by Terminal Manager
    [A] [B] [C] [D] Interview by Regional Manager
    [A] [B] [C] [D] Approval by Terminal Manager
    [A] [B] [C] [D] Approval by Regional Manager or Higher Company Official
    [A] [B] [C] [D] Verification of References
    [A] [B] [C] [D] Background Investigation
    [A] [B] [C] [D] Personality/Intelligence Test
    [A] [B] [C] [D] DOT Safety Record Verification
    [A] [B] [C] [D] ICC Permit Verification
    [A] [B] [C] [D] Polygraph Test

Does your firm hire only trained persons? Please indicate for each classification.   Y. Yes   N. No

41 [Y] [N] Drivers and Drivers' Helpers
    [Y] [N] Vehicle Repair Personnel
    [Y] [N] Dock and Warehouse Personnel
    [Y] [N] Clerical and Administrative Personnel

Would you agree that your firm has had difficulty locating trained personnel for the above occupations?

A. Strongly Agree   B. Agree   C. No Opinion   D. Disagree   E. Strongly Disagree

42 [A] [B] [C] [D] [E] Drivers and Drivers' Helpers
    [A] [B] [C] [D] [E] Vehicle Repair Personnel
    [A] [B] [C] [D] [E] Dock and Warehouse Personnel
    [A] [B] [C] [D] [E] Clerical and Administrative Personnel

Please check the appropriate box to indicate how often the workers you hire come to you with prior training from the following sources.

A. Always   B. Often   C. Occasionally   D. Never

43 [A] [B] [C] [D] Vocational school
    [A] [B] [C] [D] Military
    [A] [B] [C] [D] Training by manufacturer or vendor
    [A] [B] [C] [D] Union sponsored training
    [A] [B] [C] [D] On-the-job training with a previous employer
    [A] [B] [C] [D] Similar experience in another industry (for example, farming)
    [A] [B] [C] [D] Other

Does your firm participate in, support, or endorse any training programs administered by an employers' association or joint union-management training committee?

44 [Y] [N]

If you answered "yes" to question 44, please fill in the percentage of your nonsupervisory operating force that has received such training.

45 ☐ ☐ ☐ percent have received such training.

Do you provide your workers with any on-the-job or off-the-job instruction on your own?   Y. Yes   N. No

46 ☑Y ☑N On-the-job
   ☑Y ☑N Off-the-job

If "yes," please fill in the box(es) to indicate the percentage of your nonsupervisory operating work force who have received such training.

47 ☐ ☐ ☐ percent have received on-the-job training.
   ☐ ☐ ☐ percent have received off-the-job training.

Please indicate whether the instruction is given by: A. Your staff, or   B. Vocational schools.

48 ☑A ☑B On-the-job training
   ☑A ☑B Off-the-job training

If your firm operates a special commodity division, please indicate the percentage of these drivers who are owner-operators.

49 ☐ ☐ ☐ percent of the drivers in the special commodity division are owner-operators.

Excluding any special commodity division, what percentage of your firm's drivers are owner-operators?

50 ☐ ☐ ☐ percent.

Would you agree that since 1976 your firm has attempted to increase the percentage of its drivers who are owner-operators?
A. Strongly Agree   B. Agree   C. No Opinion   D. Disagree   E. Strongly Disagree

51 ☑A ☑B ☑C ☑D ☑E

What percentage of revenue are your firm's owner-operators normally paid?

52 ☐ ☐ ☐ percent of the revenue.

If your firm has open shop operations, please indicate whether the wage level received by the average employee in each classification is: A. less than union rate   B. equal to union rate   C. greater than union rate   D. do not know

53 ☑A ☑B ☑C ☑D Drivers and Drivers' Helpers
   ☑A ☑B ☑C ☑D Vehicle Maintenance Personnel
   ☑A ☑B ☑C ☑D Dock and Warehouse Personnel
   ☑A ☑B ☑C ☑D Clerical and Administrative Personnel

If you are an open shop employer, please indicate the approximate percentage of the nonsupervisory, operating employees in these operations whose hourly wage is as high as or higher than union scale.

54 ☐ ☐ ☐ percent have hourly wages as high as or higher than union scale.

(For all firms) Please indicate whether your firm employs part-time workers on a permanent basis.

55 ☑Y ☑N

If you answered "yes" to the previous question, how do their compensation levels compare with those of full-time employees?

56 ☑A ☑B ☑C A. Higher   B. Lower   C. About the same.

Please check the predominate method by which your over-the-road drivers are paid.

57 ☐ A. On a strictly hourly basis
   ☐ B. On a mileage basis but on an hourly basis within metropolitan areas
   ☐ C. According to established zones
   ☐ D. According to some percentage of revenue
   ☐ E. Other

If your firm has open shop operations, do these operations have assigned tractors, that is, the tractor is idle when not being used by the assigned driver?   Y. Yes   N. No

58 ☑Y ☑N

If you are an open shop employer, please check the appropriate box(es) to indicate when your over-the-road drivers receive overtime pay. (Multiple response permitted.)

59 ☐ A. After 8 hours per day
 ☐ B. After 10 hours per day
 ☐ C. After 12 hours per day
 ☐ D. After 40 hours per week
 ☐ E. After 45 hours per week
 ☐ F. After 48 hours per week
 ☐ G. After the fifth consecutive day of work
 ☐ H. After the sixth consecutive day of work
 ☐ I. On holidays
 ☐ J. Road drivers do not receive overtime pay
 ☐ K. Other

Excluding clerical and administrative employees, please indicate when your other operating, nonsupervisory employees receive overtime pay.

60   Ⓐ   Ⓑ   Ⓒ   Ⓓ   Ⓔ   Ⓕ   Ⓖ   Ⓗ   Ⓘ   Ⓙ   Ⓚ

Would you agree that graduated wage scales based on seniority are a common practice in the open shop sector?
A. Strongly Agree   B. Agree   C. No Opinion   D. Disagree   E. Strongly Disagree

61   Ⓐ   Ⓑ   Ⓒ   Ⓓ   Ⓔ

Would you agree that graduated wage scales based on seniority are more common in the open shop than in the union shop sector?
A. Strongly Agree   B. Agree   C. No Opinion   D. Disagree   E. Strongly Disagree

62   Ⓐ   Ⓑ   Ⓒ   Ⓓ   Ⓔ

If you are an open shop employer, please check the appropriate box(es) to indicate if you pay any of the following guarantees. (Multiple response permitted.)

63 ☐ A. Less than 4 hours per day call-in pay
 ☐ B. 4 hours per day call-in pay
 ☐ C. 4 hours per day once put to work
 ☐ D. 6 hours per day once put to work
 ☐ E. 8 hours once put to work
 ☐ F. 40 hours/week if eligible for the weekly guarantee
 ☐ G. 48 hours/week if eligible for the weekly guarantee
 ☐ H. More than 48 hours/week if eligible
 ☐ I. No daily guarantees
 ☐ J. No weekly guarantees
 ☐ K. Other

Please indicate the open shop employees who are eligible for the above guarantees.

64 ☐ A. Drivers and Drivers' Helpers
 ☐ B. Vehicle Repair Personnel
 ☐ C. Dock and Warehouse Personnel
 ☐ D. Clerical and Administrative Personnel

If you are an open shop employer and pay a weekly guarantee, please fill in the boxes to indicate the percentage of drivers put to work who are eligible for the weekly guarantee.

65 ☐ ☐ ☐ percent of the drivers put to work are normally eligible for the weekly guarantee.

Does your firm participate in any programs to upgrade the employment of minority or female employees?

66   Ⓨ   Ⓝ

Please fill in the boxes to indicate the racial composition of your present work force.

67 ☐ ☐ ☐ percent are Black.
 ☐ ☐ ☐ percent are Spanish-speaking.
 ☐ ☐ ☐ percent are American-Indian.
 ☐ ☐ ☐ percent are Female.

Would you agree that the percentage of minority or female employment is higher in the open shop trucking industry than in the union shop sector?
A. Strongly Agree   B. Agree   C. No Opinion   D. Disagree   E. Strongly Disagree

68   Ⓐ   Ⓑ   Ⓒ   Ⓓ   Ⓔ

If you are an open shop employer, please indicate the approximate number of workers who are eligible to receive each of the fringe benefits indicated.

A. All   B. Most   C. Few   D. None

69 [A] [B] [C] [D] Health Insurance
    [A] [B] [C] [D] Life Insurance
    [A] [B] [C] [D] Pension Plan Contributions
    [A] [B] [C] [D] Paid Vacation
    [A] [B] [C] [D] Paid Holidays
    [A] [B] [C] [D] Paid Sick Leave
    [A] [B] [C] [D] Paid Funeral Leave
    [A] [B] [C] [D] Paid Jury Duty
    [A] [B] [C] [D] Bonus or Profit-Sharing
    [A] [B] [C] [D] Moving Expenses
    [A] [B] [C] [D] Other

If you are an open shop employer, please indicate the number of paid holidays that your workers receive.

70 [ ] [ ] days.

If you are an open shop employer, please indicate in days the maximum amount of vacation that your workers can eventually earn per year, and the minimum number of years required to become eligible for this amount.

71 [ ] [ ] days' pay is the maximum amount of vacation compensation that can be earned in any given year.
    [ ] [ ] years of employment are required to earn the maximum amount of vacation compensation.

If your firm has open shop operations, please indicate whether your firm has experienced any of the following in connection with those operations. (Multiple response permitted.)

72 [ ] A. Organizing efforts but no NLRB election
    [ ] B. An NLRB election
    [ ] C. Any secondary pressure exerted on other carriers or shippers
    [ ] D. Intimidation or harassment of drivers
    [ ] E. Physical violence toward any employee
    [ ] F. Destruction of company property

Please indicate whether the Multi-Employer Pension Plan Amendments Act of 1980 has had any of the following effects on your firm's operations.   Y. Yes   N. No

73 [Y] [N] The Act has prevented my firm from merging with another firm.
    [Y] [N] The Act was an important factor in our decision to create a nonunion operation.
    [Y] [N] The Act prevented my firm from expanding.
    [Y] [N] If not for the Act, my firm would have gone out of business.

Please fill in your name and address if you wish to order the special prepublication copy of *Deregulation and Open Shop Trucking*. If you wish to remain anonymous, simply send a separate letter. You will be billed $15.00 in the spring of 1983 (List Price after publication—$27.50).

Name _____

Address _____

City _____ State _____

Zip _____

When completed, please fold in half, staple, and place in mail.

Index

STUDIES OF NEGRO EMPLOYMENT

Order from University Microfilms, Inc.
Attn: Books Editorial Department
300 North Zeeb Road
Ann Arbor, Michigan 48106

*Order this book from the Industrial Research Unit, The Wharton School, University of Pennsylvania, Philadelphia, Pennsylvania 19104

1. *The Ne*   1968
2. *The Ne*   1968
3. *The Ne*   1968
4. *The Ne*   1968
5. *The Ne*   Jr.   1969
6. *The N*
   Alan B   1969
7. *The Ne*   1969
8. *The Ne*   1969
9. *The Ne*   1970
10. *The Ne*   1970
11. *The Ne*   1970
12. *The Ne*   1970
13. *The Ne*   1970
14. *The Ne*   1970
15. *The Ne*   1970
16. *The Ne*   1971
17. *The Ne*   1970
18. *The N*   1970
19. *The Ne*   1970
20. *The Ne*   1970
21. *The N*   1970
22. *The.*   1971
23. *The.*   1971
24. *The.*   1971
25. *The*
    F. M   1972
26. *The.*
    by R   1972
27. *The.*
    and   1971
28. *The.*   1973
29. *The.*   1974
30. *The.*   1974
31. *The.*   1974

Order fr